CONTENTS

ACKNOWLEDGEMENTS

The writing of this book was greatly facilitated by a period of leave from the University of Teesside and by a Visiting Fellowship at Queen's University, Belfast.

I would especially like to thank my doctoral supervisor, Dr Michael Hart, for encouraging my interest in the enigmatic figure of Lloyd George, and Terry Jenkins for many interesting discussions on the nature of nineteenth-century Liberalism. My greatest thanks goes to Lynda for putting up with me while I was writing this book.

I am also grateful to my students at Teesside and Queen's, who have given me many opportunities to explore and refine my ideas.

INTRODUCTION

Lloyd George has not lacked biographers. Indeed, he has been one of the most closely studied of all modern British political figures and the stream of scholarship shows no signs of abating. In the last ten years there have been two excellent short surveys of his career, by Martin Pugh and Chris Wrigley, and two multi-volume appraisals, by John Grigg and Bentley Gilbert, are currently underway.[1] However, agreement about the subject of these studies seems further away than ever. For instance, while Pugh attempted to place Lloyd George within a consistent ideological framework, Wrigley preferred to examine a number of different themes in Lloyd George's career, concluding that his main aim was simply 'getting on'.[2] Similarly, Gilbert, whilst producing many interesting new appraisals of aspects of Lloyd George's career before 1914, has also been at pains to emphasise his disagreement with many of John Grigg's assessments.

This lack of unanimity is partly explained by the vastness of the topic. Lloyd George was active in politics from the mid-1880s almost up to his death in 1945. He was a Cabinet Minister for nearly 17 years and Prime Minister for almost six. His career touched on virtually every political subject of his age, from Gladstone's final years as Liberal leader to the Beveridge Report. This tends to give historians different perspectives. A scholar whose interest in Lloyd George stems from a study of his role at Versailles in 1919, will have a very different view of the 'Welsh Wizard' to someone who is mainly familiar with him as the proponent of social reform before 1914. Furthermore, the length and diversity of Lloyd George's career also means that various aspects of it are constantly subject to review and controversy. His role after 1922 was little studied until the 1970s, when it became the centre of heated debate about the validity of his proto-Keynesian proposals to tackle the Depression. Now, no picture of Lloyd George can afford to ignore his important contribution to inter-war politics, even though he never held office again after 1922. Above all, contemporaries and historians have never really succeeded in pinning down the central core of Lloyd George's beliefs, or, indeed,

1

whether he believed in anything. He has remained a remarkably elusive politician, much more so than contemporaries like Joseph Chamberlain and Winston Churchill, who also found it hard to fit into the party system.

Given this continued lack of agreement, there is room for a further short book on Lloyd George's political career, if only to summarise some of the more recent historiography. This study does not claim to have uncovered any one concept or approach that can be used to understand the 'real' Lloyd George. Rather, it aims to present Lloyd George's actions in the context of the immediate political situations within which he operated. Only thus can the remarkable twists and turns of his career be explained and some of the myths that he sedulously created about his achievements be broken down. But Lloyd George did not operate within an ideological vacuum. Throughout his political life he remained a Liberal, even if the fate of the Liberal Party was not always his first concern. This book investigates Lloyd George's relationship with Liberalism, both to provide a context for his career and as a route towards understanding some of the assumptions on which his actions were based. The resulting portrayal does not present a consistent politician, but it does show a man whose ambition was often matched by his ability, though his achievements were sometimes very different from either what he intended or claimed.

1
EARLY LIFE, 1863–1905

The first stages of David Lloyd George's life, up to his election to the House of Commons at the age of twenty-seven, have been treated in detail by many of his biographers. This interest has been prompted both by a search for the formative influences on Lloyd George's outlook and a recognition that his life was devoted to a consuming passion for politics as far back as his days as a teenage trainee solicitor in Porthmadog. But his early years have an added significance because, in his subsequent career, Lloyd George made his background an essential part of his public image and, as the occasion suited, a justification for whatever policy he was pursuing.

Lloyd George always emphasised that he was not a member of the British political elite and his rise was that of 'the cottage-bred man', as he described himself during his first election campaign in 1890, fearlessly striking down the forces of privilege.[1] But the precise meaning of this self-definition was, to say the least, flexible. To dramatise his achievements, Lloyd George often implied he had been brought up in dire poverty. He famously told a newspaper in 1898 that 'we scarcely ate fresh meat, and I remember that our greatest luxury was half an egg for each child on Sunday morning'.[2] Lloyd George even informed George Lansbury, the Labour Cabinet Minister, in 1931 that he could never betray the interests of the working class because it was 'the class from which [he] sprang'.[3] Yet, when he commented on H. H. Asquith's career in his *War Memoirs*, Lloyd George claimed they came 'from similar stock and the like environment' – thus equating himself with a man from a mill-owning family who attended a public school and Balliol College, Oxford.[4] In fact, the dimensions of the cottage in which Lloyd George was bred varied with whatever point he was making.

3

Lloyd George's background was both less romantic and more solidly middle class than he often suggested.[5] His father, William George, was the scion of Pembrokeshire farmers. After a number of false starts, including a brief study of medicine, he settled on school teaching as a career. This was one route to a geographically and socially mobile life for any ambitious young man. In 1859, when acting as headmaster of a new school in Pwllheli in North Wales, he met and married Elizabeth (Betsy) Lloyd, who was then working as a governess. Betsy's younger brother, Richard, and their mother ran a small shoe-making business in the near-by village of Llanystumdwy, employing at least two workmen. 'Uncle Richard' was later to enjoy modest fame as the alleged guide and con-science of his nephew's career. David Lloyd George was born in 1863, the second surviving child and eldest son of William and Betsy George. By then, William was the headmaster of a school in Manchester, so, ironically for such a famous Welshman, Lloyd George was born in England.

However, the family moved back to Pembrokeshire when Lloyd George was only four months old, possibly because William George's health was failing. He returned to farming, but died in 1864, leaving his wife pregnant with a further son, who was christened William in memory of his father. Betsy George had no option but to turn to her brother and mother and she went to live with them in the small house in Llanystumdwy that is now preserved as a shrine to Lloyd George. Still, she was not quite penniless. Her husband left the not inconsiderable sum of £768, most of which was probably his share of his own father's estate.[6] In addition, the Lloyds' shoe-making business seems to have been reasonably profitable and Richard Lloyd was a well-respected figure in south Caernarvon-shire, noted for his leading role in the small Nonconformist deno-mination of Campbellite Baptists.

In no sense can this be described, in the context of late-Victorian Brit-ain, as a working class or even an impoverished background, though the Lloyd family's circumstances were briefly straitened in the early 1880s when both the George brothers were training as solicitors and Richard Lloyd had retired. The capital inherited by Betsy George ensured that her two sons could embark on professional careers. Self-sacrifice and hard work were required, but this was scarcely unusual in the Victorian middle class. Lloyd George did not have to face the kind of privations endured by, for instance, Ramsay MacDonald, who was born only three years later into the rural proletariat of Scotland as the illegitimate son of a Scottish ploughman. The interest on Betsy Lloyd's capital alone prob-ably gave her an income greater than most of the agricultural labourers in

Llanystumdwy and Lloyd George's brother was keen to point out that they were much better dressed than any of the other boys at their local Church of England school.[7]

Lloyd George was a spoilt child who could do no wrong in the eyes of his uncle, mother and grandmother and this upbringing endowed him with both immense self-confidence and a permanent need for an adoring circle of admirers at home. But he was also an outstanding pupil and he and Uncle Richard quickly developed great ambitions for his future. Llanystumdwy may have been geographically isolated but Lloyd George's inheritance was far from parochial. His own father had been a man of wide interests and a friend of radical intellectuals like the Manchester Unitarian, James Martineau. William George bequeathed his son a cache of books, mainly on literature and history, which Lloyd George devoured as a child. Uncle Richard was also learned as well as pious. He carefully read a range of Nonconformist and Liberal papers each week and his workshop was the centre of village discussion of theology and politics. There was no question of attempting to tie Lloyd George to the family business. Instead, part of Betsy Lloyd's inheritance was capitalised in 1879 to article Lloyd George to the Porthmadog solicitors, Breese, Jones & Casson.

The law was the obvious profession if Lloyd George wished to rise in the world. There was little point in entering the church as his Nonconformist denomination had no paid ministers and he was too squeamish to attempt a medical career. But the law also had great advantages for an ambitious young statesman. It offered Lloyd George the chance of financial independence relatively quickly, either as a partner with his employers or by setting up on his own. Solicitors were also intimately involved in the political process as registration and election agents. Mr Breese of Lloyd George's firm was the Liberal agent in Merionethshire and south Caernarvonshire and the seventeen-year-old Lloyd George was able to play a modest role as a canvasser on the Liberal side in the 1880 elections. Whether or not he had harboured dreams of a political career when he started training as a solicitor, his exposure to public life crystallised his ambitions. On his first visit to the House of Commons in 1881, whilst in London to sit his intermediate law examinations, he recorded in his diary, 'I will not say but that I eyed the assembly in a spirit similar to that in which William the Conquerer eyed England on his visit to Edward the Confessor, the region of his future domain. Oh, vanity.'[8]

This was not just youthful boasting. Lloyd George possessed huge determination and ambition. As he rather brutally told his future wife,

'My supreme idea is to get on. To this idea I shall sacrifice everything.'[9] In the early 1880s he spent only part of his energies in qualifying as a solicitor – he barely passed with Honours in 1884. The law was merely a means to an end and he never seems to have contemplated a legal career. Most of his time went into making a name for himself as a platform orator in North West Wales, speaking at temperance meetings, in Baptist chapels and in local debating societies and building up political contacts through his legal and registration work. This experience was crucial to Lloyd George, for it convinced him, and many others, that he had a real talent for public speaking. As he noted in 1887, the most important element in furthering his political ambitions was to convince people '1st & foremost that I am a good speaker'.[10] As an impecunious young lawyer with no record of public achievement to his name, his oratory was the only asset he could offer a potential Parliamentary constituency.

Denied a partnership by his old employers, Lloyd George set up his own practice in 1885, initially from the back room of Uncle Richard's house in Criccieth, to which the old man and his family had retired in 1880. The new firm enjoyed relatively rapid growth, especially when it was joined in 1887 by William George, a much better, if less flamboyant, lawyer and businessman than his older brother. Until Lloyd George became a Minister in 1905, the family law firm was sufficiently prosperous to provide most of the income on which his political career was based, supplemented by occasional journalism and a partnership in a London law firm he helped set up in 1897.[11] While Lloyd George was always short of money, it was no mean feat to have achieved a measure of financial independence by his early twenties, as well as becoming a well-known local speaker. As early as 1886, Lloyd George seriously considered seeking the Liberal nomination for Merionethshire and he became Parliamentary candidate for Caernarvon Boroughs in 1888, when he was only twenty-five.

This was rapid progress, but it did not mean that Lloyd George was an exceptional phenomenon in Welsh politics in this period. Indeed, his background, ideas and career were fairly representative of local political trends. The 1880s were a decade of genuine political transformation in Wales, much more so than in England.[12] The dominance of the old elite of Anglicised Welsh landowners was ended decisively by the widening of the franchise in 1867 and 1884 and a new generation of MPs with less illustrious origins, proud of their Welshness and owing their allegiance to the Liberal Party, began to monopolise the representation of Wales. Some of these men had either made fortunes in business, like

D. A. Thomas of Merthyr Tydfil, or attended elite educational institutions in England, like Tom Ellis, MP for Merioneth. But others, like David Randell and Sam Evans, the new MPs elected for Gower in 1888 and Mid Glamorgan in 1890, respectively, were solicitors from modest business backgrounds, not too dissimilar to that of Lloyd George. Even his youth was not unique – Tom Ellis was twenty-seven when he became an MP, J. L. Morgan of West Carmarthen was twenty-eight and Sam Evans was thirty-one. The only thing that really marked Lloyd George out from his generation of Welsh Liberal MPs was his membership of the tiny sect of Campbellite Baptists, rather than the Calvinistic Methodists, the unofficial 'national religion' of the new Wales. Moreover, even that distinction was blurred when he married a local Methodist farmer's daughter, Margaret Owen, in 1888.

The new Welsh Liberal MPs of the late 1880s and 1890s regarded the displacement of the old elite as a national revival as well as a social revolution and they championed new policies to recognise Wales's nationhood. Most of these demands were essentially attacks on Welsh landowners and their associate, the Anglican Church of Wales, on the grounds that they were alien impositions. Foremost was the call for the disestablishment of the Church, followed by temperance reform and objections to tithe payments. Lloyd George had no problems subscribing to this programme in the 1880s. Indeed, it accurately reflected the assumptions of his own Welsh, Nonconformist background and there never seems to have been any question of his being anything other than a Liberal. The notion that he might have become a Liberal Unionist in 1886 rests heavily on the assertion of his early biographer, J. Hugh Edwards, that Lloyd George only failed to join Joseph Chamberlain's organisation because he mistook the day of the meeting in Birmingham.[13] This sounds suspiciously like later embroidery by Lloyd George himself. He may have admired Chamberlain as a fellow outsider attempting to break into the charmed circle of the Liberal leadership and the first prominent Liberal to support Welsh Church disestablishment. Certainly, Lloyd George was not alone among younger Welsh Liberals in speaking favourably of Chamberlain's decision to leave the Cabinet in March 1886 over Gladstone's decision to prefer Irish Home Rule to a measure of devolution to Ireland, Scotland and Wales. But when Chamberlain joined with the Whig landowner, Hartington, and his followers, in bringing down the Liberal government and splitting the party in June 1886, Lloyd George's enthusiasm evaporated.[14]

Lloyd George did not become noticed in North West Wales through the novelty of his politics but by articulating the standard Welsh Liberal demands and prejudices with greater vehemence and skill than many others – the classic tactic of a young man seeking to make his mark. It was the violence of his language that brought Lloyd George renown as a firebrand, rather than the originality of his ideas. As he declaimed at a meeting in honour of the Irish revolutionary, Michael Davitt, in 1886, 'Whilst working men were starving the aristocracy were feeding their game with the food that ought to go to the people' – an inflammatory sentiment, but not a policy.[15] If he did mention more extreme ideas in his speeches, like leasehold reform and land taxation, these were just extensions of the anti-landed stance of Welsh Liberals and part of a shopping list of demands to be fulfilled in the distant future after the crucial questions like disestablishment had been dealt with. Lloyd George also paid some attention to Welsh Home Rule in the later 1880s, when it was a fashionable cause among younger Welsh Liberals. However, his enthusiasm proved distinctly ephemeral and after he entered Parliament in 1890 he gave little thought to the subject until the mid-1890s.[16]

Lloyd George's career as a solicitor also offered ample opportunities for him to bring himself to public notice, mainly by accusing the landowners and publicans among the local Justices of the Peace of bias. In 1889 the whole bench of magistrates at Caernarvon walked out of court when Lloyd George accused them of prejudice in a poaching case. His most famous legal battle, though, was the 'Llanfrothen burial' furore, which 'fell like a ripe plum into the lap of the newly founded firm of Lloyd George and George' in 1888.[17] The action concerned the right of an old quarryman to be buried with Nonconformist rites in an Anglican churchyard and brought Lloyd George nation-wide publicity, especially when the local judge's hostile verdict was reversed on appeal. By 1888 he could feel he had developed enough of a reputation to win the nomination for a local Liberal seat.

And yet, selection as a Liberal candidate was not easy in North West Wales. Most MPs were unwilling to give up their safe seats until death or a lucrative post claimed them. Lloyd George was fortunate he had lived and worked all his life in or near the Caernarvon Boroughs constituency, for it was the only seat in the area where a new Liberal candidate was required in the entire period between 1886 and 1895. This was mainly because, like all the boroughs made up of groups of towns in North and Mid Wales, it was a marginal seat, not a safe Liberal bastion. In 1886 it was narrowly won by the Tories, making it the only Conservative seat in North West Wales and creating a vacancy for the post of Liberal candidate.

It became Lloyd George's prime target, especially as a borough seat would be cheaper for him to fight than any county constituency. The selection battle was long drawn out and acrimonious – something that was not unusual in Welsh seats.[18] Pwllheli, Criccieth and Nevin, the southern towns (or rather large villages) in the constituency, were won over relatively easily, but the Liberals in the much bigger northern towns of Caernarvon, Conway and Bangor were less easily convinced. All these towns had a significant English-speaking middle-class element, a strong drink lobby and powerful Anglican connections, centred on Bangor Cathedral. Local Liberals feared Lloyd George's extreme reputation would scare off uncommitted and moderate voters. It was not until the Llanfrothen burial case made him a national figure and all other plausible candidates had withdrawn that Lloyd George was finally accepted by the northern towns.

Lloyd George had a further stroke of luck in 1890 when the sitting Tory MP died, precipitating a by-election. The Liberals were benefiting from a national swing against the Tory government and victory was widely predicted in the Liberal press. The new Conservative candidate was the squire of Llanystumdwy, H. J. E. Nanney, and Lloyd George was eager to present the contest as the new Wales against the old, democracy against aristocracy. But it soon became clear, even to his most committed supporters, that the election would be very close and Lloyd George had to moderate his rhetoric during the campaign and concentrate on a sober presentation of the Welsh Liberal pieties of temperance and Church disestablishment. The controversy surrounding his extreme reputation ensured the poll increased by 11.2 per cent over the 1886 turnout, but Lloyd George only scraped home by 18 votes, on a swing of less than 2 per cent.

The seat remained marginal until 1906, when Lloyd George had established himself as the most prominent Welsh politician and unofficial leader of Welsh Liberalism and Nonconformity. In the 1890s he had to spend a good deal of time in the Commons promoting causes of interest to the Caernarvon Boroughs on subjects as diverse as fishing rights, railway rates and the appointment of Welsh-speaking judges, (though he refused to open constituency mail) while William George looked after local organisation. Money remained a constant difficulty and the 1892 election was financed with a bank overdraft.[19] But the crucial factor was that Lloyd George won and held his seat when only twenty-seven years old. This allowed him to embark on a Parliamentary career at the same age as the most privileged scions of the aristocracy.

Just as Lloyd George had made an early impression on the political world of North West Wales, he lost no time in embarking on the conquest of the national political stage. This involved him in the first stages of his long and tortuous relationship with the political demands of his own Welsh nation. At different times over the next 15 years, depending on the political situation, Lloyd George was both to aspire to the political leadership of Wales and to seek recognition as a British politician. The two aims, though, were not necessarily incompatible and Lloyd George managed to achieve both by 1905. But from the first, Wales was never enough for him. His aim was nothing less than the British Cabinet and his attitude to Welsh demands depended on whether they would help or hinder his arrival at that eminence. He certainly made it clear as early as possible that he did not wish to confine himself to Welsh affairs. In the Commons he harried the Tory government of Lord Salisbury, particularly by combining with another new Welsh MP, Sam Evans, in raising innumerable difficulties over the Tithe Rent Charges (Recovery) Bill and the Clergy Discipline Bill.[20] These were essentially trivial exercises, but they at least brought him to the attention of the Liberal leaders in the Commons and showed he had worked hard at learning the rules of Parliamentary procedure. Outside of Westminster he deliberately sought and accepted invitations to speak all over England, mainly on Nonconformist matters. His first great success was at a temperance meeting in Manchester on 4 June 1890 and by October he was writing 'with the exception of one week reserved for my constituents, all my time is taken up with addressing meetings in England'.[21]

This success was not achieved without much labour and careful deliberation. In Parliament Lloyd George was anxious not to speak either too often or on subjects on which he could not make a telling contribution. All his early speeches were rehearsed beforehand, and often illustrated with apt references he had unearthed from Hansard and the Blue Books. Quickly, a distinctive Lloyd George style became noticeable, mixing hard-won information with humour, sentiment and invective. It was typical that the speaker Lloyd George most admired was the Irishman, Tim Healy, who was noted for his rudeness, but also for his ability to hold an audience and make his points hit home.[22] Rudeness was essential to Lloyd George's style, too. A good early example was his criticism of various items of state expenditure on ceremony in 1890:

> With regard to the first payment, namely £439 3s. 4d., fees paid on the Installation of H.R.H. Prince Henry of Prussia as a Knight of the Garter,

I wish to point out that that dignity is, as a general rule granted for
some signal service rendered to the country; but what service has
Prince Henry of Prussia ever rendered to this country? He has not yet
rendered any service to his own country, to say nothing of service to
Great Britain...With regard to the second item, £2,769 4s. 8d. Equi-
page money on appointment of the Earl of Zetland Lord Lieutenant of
Ireland, I think it is generally admitted that this office is a sinecure....
We have frequently been reminded by the Chief Secretary that he is
the real governor of Ireland. The Lord Lieutenant is simply a man in
buttons, who wears silk stockings and has a coat of arms on his car-
riage.[23]

By 1892 he had made a mark as a critic of the government and a master of
invective, in the Commons and on the public platform. He was not
regarded, nor did he wish to be, as a constructive thinker. Nor did he aspire
at this time to be the leading figure in Welsh Liberalism. That niche was
already filled by Tom Ellis (only four years older than Lloyd George),
who had established his reputation by brokering the 1889 Welsh Intermediate Education Act and by philosophising on Welsh culture. In fact,
Lloyd George was distinctly unpopular with many Welsh Liberal MPs,
who regarded his undisguised ambition with distrust.

The 1892 election returned a minority Liberal government under
Gladstone, dependent on Irish Nationalist support. Ellis's role as the
most effective of the Welsh MPs was confirmed when he was appointed
to the whips office – a clear recognition of the significance of the Welsh
Liberal bloc of 31 MPs, when the government had only 43 more MPs
than the Tories. As Lloyd George no longer had a Tory government to
criticise, he was temporarily reduced to obscurity on the Liberal backbenches. However, the new political situation presented him with fresh
opportunities, as, despite various concessions to Welsh feeling, the
Welsh MPs were increasingly dissatisfied with the Liberal government's
performance. The Parliamentary timetable was dominated by Irish
Home Rule, while their central demand for Church disestablishment
languished. Increasingly, the Welsh MPs demanded that disestablishment should become the government's second priority after Home
Rule. The Cabinet were not enthusiastic and no Bill appeared in 1893.
The Welsh then learned that while disestablishment would be introduced in the 1894 session, it would have no chance of passing even the
Commons as it was ranked lower than the Irish Evicted Tenants Bill and
various electoral reforms.

Lloyd George recognised that this situation offered the chance to create a new power base for himself as the leading figure in Welsh Liberalism. This post was vacant, as Ellis was silenced by his role in the government, where he became Chief Whip in 1894. Moreover, the new chairman of the Welsh Liberal MPs, Sir George Osborne Morgan, was an elderly figure with no pretence to dominate his colleagues. In a suitably dramatic gesture Lloyd George resigned the Liberal Whip, and he was soon joined by three of his colleagues, D. A. Thomas, Herbert Lewis and Frank Edwards, in the 'Revolt of the Four'. They demanded disestablishment should be passed by the Commons that year, if necessary in an autumn session. Yet, Lloyd George's actions revealed his ambition rather than his single-minded devotion to the cause of Wales. He had helped defeat a similar rebellion the previous year, probably because it was instigated by his rival, D. A. Thomas, and, in turn, Thomas only joined Lloyd George in 1894 to prevent himself being outflanked.

The 'Four's' revolt created intense disagreements among the Welsh Liberal MPs. It also lost most of its point in February 1895 when the government reintroduced its Disestablishment Bill at the head of its programme. Lloyd George was reduced to insisting the government set up a Welsh National Council to administer the Church's endowments, rather than a group of commissioners. Thomas saw his chance to challenge Lloyd George for the leadership of the rebels and proposed the income of the disendowed church should be distributed to the Welsh County Councils in proportion to their population, thus favouring the South Wales counties of Glamorgan and Monmouth – a proposal that was vigorously resisted by MPs from the more thinly populated counties of North and Mid Wales (including Lloyd George). Thus the revolt was in severe difficulties by mid-1895 when the exhausted Liberal government finally collapsed and was defeated in a General Election. The bitter splits within Welsh Liberalism remained, though, with Lloyd George writing that his fellow MPs were 'green with envy and spite. Many a bilious attack is fermenting in their greedy stomachs.'[24] He was soon being accused by enemies like Bryn Roberts, MP for Caernarvonshire, of bringing the Liberal government down by his antics in the Commons.

However, Lloyd George displayed a tactic that was to become typical in his later career. Instead of retreating, he responded to a difficult situation by attack. He had taken the initiative in August 1894 in founding an organisation called Cymru Fydd ('The Wales that is to be'). Its policies included the usual Welsh Liberal nostrums plus Home Rule for Wales – something that Lloyd George had not paid much attention to since

1889–90. The inaction of the Westminster Parliament had disillusioned some Welsh Liberals and this feeling made Cymru Fydd's espousal of Home Rule briefly popular in the mid-1890s. The real object of Cymru Fydd, though, did not lie in the realm of policy. Its aim was to amalgamate with (i.e. take over) the existing Liberal Federations in North and South Wales, forming a new Welsh Liberal organisation, dominated by Lloyd George and his allies. As such, it was the complement in the country of the Revolt of the Four in Parliament. In the autumn of 1895, Lloyd George turned his energies to Cymru Fydd with renewed vigour in an effort to conquer Welsh Liberalism despite his setbacks in the Commons. The key to his campaign was the South Wales Liberal Federation and, for the first time, Lloyd George campaigned intensively in the mining and industrial centres of South Wales. He did not like what he saw. The population was not really Welsh at all, but 'semi-English' – 'Newport Englishmen' as he called them in horror – and sunk in 'morbid footballism'.[25] There was little wish to join an organisation dominated by men from the North and West. D. A. Thomas was well aware of this and he ensured that a suitably packed meeting of the South Wales Liberal Federation at Newport howled down Lloyd George's proposal to merge with Cymru Fydd in January 1896.

This was a decisive defeat for Lloyd George, ending his attempt to forge Welsh Liberalism into a disciplined party under his command. But he was not too distraught. His commitment to Welsh Home Rule had been purely tactical and he could easily return to the wider field of British politics to pursue his career, especially as there was now a Tory government for him to attack. With Cymru Fydd he was probably seeking to achieve the impossible. Welsh Liberals were never likely to unite behind Home Rule. The Liberals of South Wales, for instance, lived in an economy and society far more closely linked to England and the Empire than to the rest of Wales.[26] Later on, however eminent Lloyd George became, it was notable that his prestige in South Wales always remained conditional and circumscribed.

When Lloyd George returned to the subject of Welsh Liberal organisation in 1897–8 it was with a more modest proposal for a Welsh National Liberal Council – purely a talking shop for constituency delegates.[27] This idea was successful and had the added bonus of isolating D. A. Thomas, who was seen to be unreasonable in refusing to co-operate with so innocuous a development. The widespread acceptance of the Council was symbolic of Lloyd George's growing significance in Welsh Liberalism, once he had realised the limits of what could be achieved. When the chairmanship of Welsh Liberalism became vacant again in 1898, Lloyd George refused to allow his name to go forward, even though he might well have won the post. Instead, his friend and ally, Alfred Thomas of Pontypridd, was elected, Lloyd George deciding to reserve himself for 'bigger work in which I could take a leading part'.[28] He did not need to seek the formal leadership of so fractious a body as Welsh Liberalism, where he already had several implacable enemies. He preferred to aim for the kind of loose supremacy that Ellis had enjoyed in the late 1880s.

This transformation in Lloyd George's standing with his colleagues by 1898 was largely the result of his increased prestige in the Liberal Parliamentary Party as a whole. The Liberal leadership of the late 1890s, under Rosebery, Sir William Harcourt and then Sir Henry Campbell-Bannerman, was notoriously divided and ineffective. Lloyd George was one of the few backbenchers who filled the vacuum left by the leaders and he greatly enhanced his reputation in the Commons by leading a series of ferocious assaults on the Tory government that was returned to power in 1895. He had particular success in abusing the 1896 Agricultural Rating Bill, which relieved farm land of some of its liability for rates. The Liberals were in a somewhat awkward position on this Bill. Most of their supporters hated it as a subsidy that would ultimately end up in landlords' pockets, but it would obviously be very popular with farmers. Lloyd George skirted this problem by attacking the Bill as a measure that would personally benefit leading Tories. He claimed that Henry Chaplin, the Minister responsible for the measure, would benefit by £700 a year and the Tory Cabinet by a capital value of £2.25 million.[29]

These assaults embarrassed the government and Lloyd George was suitably rewarded. He was asked to help lead the Liberals' criticism of measures like the 1897 Voluntary Schools Bill and in 1897–8 he started to talk of himself, and to be talked about, as a future member of the Cabinet.[30] In the country, too, he became better-known as a speaker in demand on Liberal platforms. But in all these activities, Lloyd George's emphasis, as in 1890–2, was on attacking whatever the Conservatives were doing. He said very little about what a Liberal government would do, beyond the standard Welsh Liberal programme of the 1880s. Most importantly for his future career, there is very little evidence that Lloyd George was influenced by, or even much aware of, the new thinking on social reform occurring in Liberalism, even though he was a friend of the New Liberal journalist, H. G. Massingham, from the mid-1890s. When Lloyd George read the *Fabian Essays* of 1889, the only item he found of interest was the church attendance figures.[31] The sole measure of social reform he took to including in his speeches was old age pensions, and this was largely because he could attack Chamberlain for promising them in 1895 and then reneging on his commitment. But nor was there any indication that Lloyd George was hostile to state action to benefit the poor. His speeches were full of contrasts of the wealth and privilege of landowners and royalty with the poverty of the many. In 1890, when he had attacked state expenditure on ceremonial, he had pointed to the report of the Commons committee on sweated industries, claiming that expenditure on superfluous display was directly responsible for the misery of the piece workers who supplied luxuries. If the rich were responsible for at least some poverty, it was a fairly short step to expecting them to contribute to its alleviation.

By 1898 Lloyd George was definitely one of the coming men of Parliamentary Liberalism, and the Cymru Fydd fiasco was an increasingly distant memory. This status was eventually confirmed by his role in opposing the Boer War, which broke out in 1899, though both Lloyd George and his party suffered greatly in the short term. The war bitterly divided Liberalism for three years, substantially widening the gap between Liberal Imperialists and Radicals. The first group wished to develop Liberals' enthusiasm for the Empire and an active foreign policy and drop or downgrade unpopular 'fads' like Irish Home Rule. Radicals, on the other hand, disliked jingoism and wished to defend their party's commitment to the full programme of late nineteenth-century Liberalism. Hitherto, Lloyd George had said little on foreign and Imperial questions. Now, however, he unhesitatingly condemned the government's actions, lining himself up against the Liberal Imperialists led by Rosebery, Asquith, Haldane and Grey. The determining factor for Lloyd George, though, was the necessity to continue attacking the government, whatever it did, rather than a commitment to a Radical foreign policy. He believed that the war was a huge blunder that would discredit the government and the Liberals could only benefit from attacking the enterprise. 'I believe their downfall is assured,' he told his wife. 'If they go on the war will be so costly in blood and treasure as to sicken the land. If they withdraw they will be laughed out of power.'[32] His stance did not imply he was opposed to the existence, or even the expansion, of the Empire where this was in British interests. But he was against what he regarded as an unnecessary war, started by Tory politicians for their own ends.

Lloyd George was not above downplaying his stance on the war when this was essential, as it was in his own constituency in the 1900 General

Election, when he feared losing his seat – the Lloyd family had been
burnt in effigy at Criccieth on Mafeking night.[33] Nor did he cut all links
with Rosebery. But he was one of the most outspoken and wounding critics of the government's policies. In particular, he delivered a series of
stinging attacks on Joseph Chamberlain, alleging in a famous exchange
in the Commons on 10 December 1900, that he and his family were making money from government contracts to supply the troops.[34] It was
these assaults that first made Lloyd George a well-known public figure. It
became worthwhile for Tory Ministers and journalists to revile him in
their speeches and hold him up as a dread example of the extremism and
irresponsibility of the Liberal opposition. Lloyd George almost lost his
life when he attempted to address a meeting in Chamberlain's fortress of
Birmingham and the platform was stormed by an angry mob. The London side of his legal work suffered a boycott that seriously damaged his
finances, and his elder son, Richard, had to be withdrawn from his English
public school because of the bullying provoked by his father's stance on
the war.[35] This was a high price to pay, but Lloyd George's courage and
persistence made him a standard-bearer of the Liberal Radicals who
opposed the war. His standing as a potential Cabinet Minister was confirmed as he would evidently be too dangerous to exclude from any future
Liberal Cabinet, even, perhaps, one led by the Imperialist Rosebery.

The Boer War ensured Lloyd George could finally break away from
his roots as a purely Welsh politician to become a significant figure in the
Liberal leadership. Alone of the Welsh MPs he was a serious contender
for high office in a future Liberal government. Ironically, though, his status within the wider Liberal Party further reinforced his unofficial role as
the leader of Welsh Liberalism. This became very apparent in 1902 when
the Tories faced uproar over their new Education Act.[36] Lloyd George
was not instinctively hostile to this Act at first, but it soon became clear
that many Nonconformists interpreted it as forcing local authorities to
subsidise ailing Church of England schools. This was greatly resented in
a largely Nonconformist country like Wales.

Some English Nonconformists responded to the Act by refusing to pay
rates. But Lloyd George suggested a far more co-ordinated policy to
Welsh Liberals at a conference of local authorities in Cardiff in 1903. He
proposed that they should concentrate on winning majorities in all the
Welsh County Councils in the 1904 elections. Then they should refuse
any rate aid to Anglican schools, ostensibly on the grounds that they were
in poor repair. This might just be legal. Lloyd George hoped to force the
Church to agree to a compromise, probably involving local authority

control of teaching appointments in their schools in return for the restoration of rate support.[37] It was a remarkable tribute to the ingenuity of Lloyd George's scheme and his own prestige in Wales that his plan was adopted by all but a handful of Welsh Liberals. They duly went on to win control of every County Council in 1904 and to implement his idea.

Meanwhile, Lloyd George engaged in lengthy discussions in 1903–5 with the Bishop of St Asaph to explore the possibilities of a deal. This process revealed the flaw in Lloyd George's scheme, for he had no more than a moral authority over his followers and elements in the Church felt it could rely on government backing. He could not, therefore, force the two old enemies of Church and Chapel to any sort of accommodation. But these events revealed for the first time that Lloyd George's ambitions reached beyond just being a critic of other people's measures. He wanted to solve the Welsh education dispute, rather than parade the Nonconformist viewpoint. However, in the absence of any agreement, the government passed the Education (Local Authorities Default) Act in 1904, which allowed them to pay rate aid directly to Church schools and deduct the sum from the state's grant to defaulting councils. In return, Lloyd George threatened that any council penalised by the Act would organise a withdrawal of all children from Church schools in its area. There the matter rested until the Conservative government fell in December 1905. The Board of Education only penalised three councils for relatively small sums and there were no mass withdrawals of children. Effectively a draw was obtained between the government and Welsh Liberalism.

The Welsh revolt made Lloyd George the most prominent Nonconformist politician in Britain. In 1904 he found himself invited to stay with both Rosebery and Campbell-Bannerman and consulted by the opposition front bench over tactics on all issues affecting Nonconformists, like the 1904 Licensing Act.[38] Meanwhile, the Education Act had precipitated a slide in the government's popularity, accelerated by its divisions over Chamberlain's plans for tariff reform, announced in 1903. The defence of free trade reunited the Liberals and established the Imperialist Asquith as the heir-apparent to the ageing Radical Campbell-Bannerman. But Lloyd George had installed himself as an indispensable lieutenant. By this time he was popular not only with Nonconformists and Welshmen, but also with some of the younger Liberals who favoured new ideas about social reform and gathered around H. G. Massingham at the Liberal weekly *The Speaker*, soon to be renamed the *Nation*. They admired his stance over the Boer War and, increasingly, they came to see him as a possible ally in office, however nineteenth century his Radicalism might

seem. In 1905, though, Lloyd George's image with the public and his
fellow politicians was uncomplicated, for perhaps the last time in his life.
He was seen as a Radical, committed to the old shibboleths of peace,
retrenchment and reform; the champion of Nonconformity and Welsh
nationhood and foe of the old enemies of privilege and priesthood. The
next ten years were to change this image out of all recognition, but this
was something nobody could have predicted in 1905.

2

NEW LIBERAL, 1905–14

The Tory government led by Arthur Balfour finally resigned in November 1905. It was on the brink of disintegration anyway over its disagreements on tariff reform and Balfour hoped to exploit the continuing divisions in Liberalism between the Imperialists and Radicals, by challenging Sir Henry Campbell-Bannerman to form an effective Cabinet that could unite his party. After a brief struggle, the new Prime Minister was successful, forming a carefully balanced administration that included all the leading Imperialists bar Rosebery. Lloyd George did not join in the frenzied attempts of many of his colleagues to beg office, by letter or in person. He simply assumed he would be offered a post, even neglecting to tell Campbell-Bannerman of his whereabouts in London.[1] Despite Liberalism's ten years out of office, most of the places in the new Cabinet were reserved for men who had played some role in the last government of 1895. Only six of Campbell-Bannerman's Cabinet had never held any ministerial post before and Lloyd George was the youngest of them, confirming his role as a rising star in the party.

There are some indications that Lloyd George would have liked to be Home Secretary, with a brief to introduce Welsh Church disestablishment.[2] But Campbell-Bannerman never considered him for more than a minor office, finally settling on President of the Board of Trade as a suitable starting point for such an unknown quantity. Lloyd George could, therefore, do little to implement the Welsh political programme, even after the expected Liberal landslide was achieved in the 1906 General Election. Disestablishment was shunted off to a Royal Commission. But, by achieving Cabinet office, he gained official sanction for his role as leader of Welsh Liberalism. To confirm this, the other Welshman to obtain a post was his crony Herbert Lewis, at the whips office. Effectively, Lloyd

George struck a deal with the Liberal leadership. He was expected to head off Welsh dissatisfaction with the government, especially over the non-appearance of disestablishment. This was not always an easy task and Lloyd George had to produce one of his best rhetorical performances to persuade a Welsh Liberal convention at Cardiff on 10 October 1907 to be patient. In return, the Welsh received a number of administrative concessions, most importantly a separate Welsh Department of Education in 1907. To help him keep the Welsh Liberals in line, Lloyd George was also allowed a central role in dispensing government patronage, from Lord Lieutenancies to judgeships, in Wales.[3] Old friends, like D. R. Daniel, who became second secretary to a Royal Commission, were suitably rewarded and enemies anathematised.

But Lloyd George's main task was to prove himself to his Cabinet colleagues as a competent administrator at the Board of Trade. Here he succeeded in achieving a solid, if unspectacular, legislative record, skilfully piloting the Board's proposals like the Merchant Shipping Act and Patents Act through the Commons and laying the groundwork for a Port of London Act in 1908. Previously, Lloyd George had been known as a rebel. At the Board of Trade he revealed unexpected talents as a conciliator, especially over the Merchant Shipping Act. He consulted the shipowners before the Bill was introduced and adapted it in response to their representations as it proceeded through the Commons. The result was a careful compromise between all the parties involved. He also achieved some well-publicised success in averting a railway strike in 1907, by mediating between the owners and the union.

This sort of activity might have been fairly mundane, but in a way this benefited Lloyd George because it helped erase his previous reputation as a 'wild man' and replace it with the image of a sober, respectable statesman. Moreover, it proved to be a distinct advantage to be at a relatively obscure department in 1906–8, because the government's record was so poor on many of its major pieces of legislation. Lloyd George at least escaped any responsibility for such disasters as the 1906 Education Bill, the 1907 Irish Councils Bill and the 1908 Licensing Bill, none of which became law, either because they collapsed under their own unpopularity or were blocked by the Tory-dominated House of Lords. Thus, when a Cabinet reshuffle became unavoidable on Campbell-Bannerman's resignation in 1908, Lloyd George could hope for promotion.

The most important post that became free in 1908 was that of Chancellor of the Exchequer, vacated when Asquith succeeded Campbell-Bannerman as Prime Minister. It was likely it would be given to a Radical, rather than an Imperialist, to balance Asquith's new role as Prime Minister. The most senior Radical was John Morley, but he was too old and prone to threaten resignation to be considered (though Asquith seems to have mentioned the matter to him out of courtesy). Lloyd George, on the other hand, was popular with many Liberals and had proved his ability at the Board of Trade. In particular, his promotion might placate the powerful Nonconformist element in the party who were increasingly frustrated with the failure of legislation on education and licensing. This factor was probably decisive in ensuring Lloyd George was promoted to the Exchequer.

Lloyd George was understandably gleeful, informing his brother that he was now 'second in Command in the Liberal host' – something more senior colleagues like Morley, Grey, Crewe and Loreburn would scarcely have accepted.[4] It was not clear, though, that his appointment would lead to any great changes. Most importantly, there was no real indication in 1908 that Lloyd George had plans to promote large-scale expenditure on anything, including social reform. He had been notably cautious during the 1906 election campaign, failing even to definitely promise old age pensions in his speeches.[5] The new Cabinet Minister who was associated with social reform in 1908 was Winston Churchill, Lloyd George's successor at the Board of Trade and author of the challenging article, 'The Untrodden Field of Politics' in the *Nation* on 7 March 1908.

If anything, Lloyd George was expected to put a brake on his colleagues' spending plans, especially at the Admiralty. In fact, that was the role he initially attempted to play. The 1908 Budget had already been prepared by Asquith, so Lloyd George had nearly a year to prepare his first financial package. It soon became apparent to him that Asquith had escaped from the Treasury just in time to preserve his reputation as a stern financier. Asquith had been able to reduce indirect taxation and the national debt by cutting military spending for two years, but he had also agreed in 1908 to introduce old age pensions and pressure was mounting to increase naval expenditure to keep ahead of the German Navy. Both were expensive commitments and a deficit of over £16 million was forecast for 1909. The legislation for pensions had been prepared by Asquith and Lloyd George had no option but to introduce it. He made some real efforts to scale down or at least delay naval expenditure in 1908–9, including an attempt to explore a truce with Germany in a rather ill-judged visit to the Continent, but to no avail. The Imperialists in the Cabinet were determined and had the backing of the Prime Minister. By autumn 1908 Lloyd George was reconciled to making large tax increases in his first Budget.[6]

The implications of this situation were alarming. The government had endured a slump in its popularity in 1907–8, regularly losing by-elections. The ineffectual nature of its legislative programme prompted speculation that the Cabinet might simply expire, as the last Liberal government had in 1895. The last thing it needed was a Budget involving heavy tax rises. However, the outline of how this might be achieved was already apparent to Lloyd George in previous Liberal policy. He could meet part of the deficit by raising indirect taxes on alcohol and tobacco, but direct taxation would have to provide at least some of the new revenue. Harcourt's 1894 Budget had shown how this might be done by graduating death duties, i.e. levying higher rates of taxation on greater wealth. Asquith had expanded this idea in his 1907 Budget by reducing income tax on earned incomes under £2000, but not on incomes above this figure. So the obvious strategy for Lloyd George was to raise taxation rates for higher income groups. Asquith had considered a supertax on the wealthy for his 1907 Budget, for instance, and Lloyd George included it in his 1909 Budget at 6d in the pound on incomes over £5000 – a measure that affected only about 12 000 earners. He also raised income tax to 1s 6d on incomes over £3000 and introduced a higher scale of death duties. The vast majority of the million or so income tax payers, who lived on earned incomes under £2000, continued to pay only 9d income tax and many benefited from the introduction of child rebates.

The difficulty with such an approach, ingenious though it was in ensuring most income tax payers were not affected by rises in direct taxes, was that it was scarcely exciting, or calculated to recover the government's popularity. While pensions were presumably popular with many working-class Liberals, they might well dislike any increases in indirect taxes. Moreover, the announcement of old age pensions in 1908 had done nothing to revive the government's fortunes at by-elections.[7] Middle-class Liberals, on the other hand, might dislike pensions and be fearful about any tendency to increase direct taxes. Radical Liberals of all classes would be offended by increased naval spending. Such a Budget would scarcely rescue the party's fortunes, or make Lloyd George a popular Chancellor. However, he had no intention of merely accepting this situation and apologising for his difficulties. As always, he responded to a crisis by going on the offensive. The key was to find a way of uniting Liberals behind the Budget and simultaneously launching an assault on the Tories. By September 1908 Lloyd George was considering the possibility of doing all this by including a range of land taxes and a valuation of all British land in the Budget.[8] Eventually, four minor duties were proposed, on land leases, unearned increments in land values, undeveloped land and mineral rights. Lloyd George did not hope to raise a great deal of revenue from this route, possibly as little as £500 000 in the first year. But he did hope to produce a political storm.

An essential part of the Welsh Liberal creed was an intense dislike of landlords, as alien tyrants and allies of the Church. But there is no need to see the decision to include land taxation in the 1909 Budget as merely the expression of Lloyd George's deeply held childhood beliefs, or as something that was irrelevant to an urbanised society. Rather, the formation of the 1909 Budget was a response to the specific political situation in Britain in 1908–9. The Tories were no longer an overwhelmingly landed party, but landowners were still a significant force in Conservatism, providing many of the party's leaders, over a quarter of its MPs and financing and leading many constituency parties.[9] Above all, the House of Lords, still made up largely of major landowners, was a crucial element in Tory Party strategy. In 1906–8 it was used to great effect to block legislation of interest to Liberal supporters, but which was not popular with most voters, including proposals on education, temperance and Scottish land reform. Not surprisingly, many Liberals had come to see landowners as the authors of all their misfortunes and any direct attack on them would be welcomed with enthusiasm. It might also distract attention from many of the less palatable features of the Budget, giving at least the impression that much of the new revenue was to be raised by soaking reactionary landlords. Such a strategy would be reinforced by the likely reaction of the Tory Party. They would hate any idea of land taxation as a vindictive assault on an interest dear to their own hearts. If they directed their attacks on the land taxes, Liberals too might focus on them and they would at least know they had hit home against the enemy. Moreover, as, by convention, the Lords did not interfere with the Budget, the Tories would not be able to prevent this assault on 'privilege'.

This was an ingenious use of the Budget as a political strategy, rather than just a method of balancing the country's books, but it also had important consequences for Liberalism. Rather than reining in expenditure and seeking to lower taxes, Lloyd George had decided to develop a strategy whereby the state's tax base could be greatly expanded by increasing graduated taxes on incomes and estates at death. Liberalism was no longer to be the party of retrenchment. This was a decision that was forced on him, but once taken he embraced it wholeheartedly. It meant that in the future, Liberals would be able to finance other social reforms apart from old age pensions and to develop a whole new social programme. It also meant they had the means to defeat the Tory allegation that tariffs would be necessary to finance the state's future expenditure. Free trade was safe – another means of selling the Budget to Liberals. None of these startling new developments could have been predicted from an examination of Lloyd George's previous career. They were not the outcome of long-held beliefs, but of a unique open-mindedness and daring when faced by a desperate political situation.

Lloyd George was able to make new departures as Chancellor at least partly because he refused to be imprisoned by the routine of his office or by the advice of his senior officials. Indeed, it was while he was Chancellor that his unique style of working started to evolve. This was largely the consequence of his dislike of lengthy official memoranda and regular office hours. His junior Minister, Charles Hobhouse, was soon complaining that Lloyd George 'will look at no papers, and do no office work'.[10] Instead, Lloyd George mixed relaxation and work in a way that was disconcerting to many civil servants. Their chief preferred to discuss ideas face to face, often on the golf course or at the working breakfasts that became a regular feature of life at No. 11 Downing Street.[11] Nor did he rely on the leading civil servants of his own department for advice. He preferred to develop the outline of a strategy himself and then flesh out the details in discussion with anyone he felt was useful or knowledgeable. Thus on the Budget, Lloyd George knew his senior officials, like Sir George Murray, the Permanent Secretary, disliked the new direction he was contemplating, so he avoided them and used political allies like C. F. G. Masterman and Rufus Isaacs, more junior Treasury officials, like John Bradbury, and civil servants from the Inland Revenue, especially Robert Chalmers, to develop his plans. Both his ideas and his novel methods outraged many of his officials and his own deputy, Charles Hobhouse, who did not hesitate to complain to Asquith that Lloyd George 'will neither give nor receive advice, and regards Murray and myself as mere marplots'.[12]

This was merely a foretaste of the reaction the Budget received in the Cabinet, where no fewer than 14 meetings were devoted to its proposals. Probably three-quarters of the Cabinet had serious reservations about the Budget.[13] Ironically for Lloyd George, the attack was led by the Cabinet's Radicals – the section with whom he was publicly associated. Men like Reginald McKenna, John Morley, Lord Loreburn, Lewis Harcourt and John Burns had opposed the imperialism of the Boer War, but they also disliked rising public expenditure and taxation, especially when some of it was destined for more armaments. Allied to these feelings was a general distaste for Lloyd George's methods. They all felt that he was not the stern figure of financial discipline a Chancellor should be and that he had manipulated the figures to overestimate the potential deficit and need for new taxes. Asquith humoured Morley by summing up this view in a rhyme:

> George moves in a mysterious way,
> His little sums to make;
> Loose logic, lax arithmetic
> Contribute to the fake...[14]

Ironically, Lloyd George had to rely on some (though not all) of the Liberal Imperialists in the Cabinet, primarily Carrington, Churchill, Haldane and, above all, Asquith, to force the Budget through. They accepted the need for new taxes for the Navy and were less hostile to a greater role for the state in social reform. This new configuration was of great significance. Previously, the main division in Liberalism had been between Radicals and Imperialists. After 1909 a new split appeared, cutting across the old lines, between those who supported or opposed higher taxation and social reform.

In all this, the support of Asquith was crucial. He recognised the need for a great gesture to revive Liberal enthusiasm and attack the Tories. The alternative was more years of defeat and then disintegration. Obviously, some moderate Liberals might be scared off by the Budget, but there were clear signs in the by-election results that the Liberals had already lost much of the middle-class support they had temporarily won from the Tories in 1906. They had nothing to lose by gambling on the Budget. Moreover, the discussions of 1909 marked the real beginning of the Asquith–Lloyd George partnership that was effectively to dominate Liberalism down to 1914. Asquith chaired the Cabinet and dealt with the most delicate 'high political' negotiations over central problems like the constitutional crisis of 1910–11 and Home Rule in 1913–14. Lloyd George provided the ideas for the party's direction and the oratorical fireworks in the country. It was a peculiarly powerful team and it was responsible for most of Liberalism's great achievements in the Edwardian era.

Lloyd George's Budget speech in May 1909 was rather inept, probably because he was tied to a lengthy and technical script. But the reaction

to his new initiative fulfilled all his hopes.[15] Some moderate Liberals
were appalled, but their numbers were relatively few. Most were
delighted by the Budget's boldness and especially by the assault on landowners embodied in the land taxes. The Tories were, naturally, furious.
Protest meetings were organised in the City and apoplectic comments
by a variety of peers received widespread publicity. The Conservatives,
as Lloyd George had hoped, concentrated much of their fire on the land
taxes, which were obstructed in committee in the Commons for 22 days,
and not passed until 1 September 1909. In the country there were
increasing signs of a Liberal revival in morale and popularity and the party
held four seats in by-elections in mid-1909, reversing the trend of
1907–8.[16]

This encouraged Lloyd George into his second great departure of
1909. In a series of speeches, most notably at Limehouse on 30 July
1909 and at Newcastle on 9 October, he in effect declared class war on
landowners and the House of Lords. They were accused of being a
group of parasites, leeching revenue from the rest of society – men
without special talent or merit who wielded inordinate power. At Newcastle he threatened that if the Lords tried to obstruct the Budget:

> They are forcing a revolution, and they will get it. The Lords may
> decree a revolution, but the people will direct it. ...The question will be
> asked whether five hundred men, ordinary men chosen accidentally
> from among the unemployed, should override the judgement – the
> deliberate judgement – of millions of people who are engaged in the
> industry which makes the wealth of the country.
>
> That is one question. Another will be, Who ordained that a few
> should have the land of Britain as a perquisite? Who made ten thousand
> people owners of the soil, and the rest of us trespassers in the land of our
> birth? Who is it who is responsible for the scheme of things whereby
> one man is engaged through life in grinding labour to win a bare and
> precarious subsistence for himself, and when, at the end of his days, he
> claims at the hands of the community he served a poor pension of eight
> pence a day, he can only get it through a revolution, and another man
> who does not toil receives every hour of the day, every hour of the
> night, whilst he slumbers, more than his poor neighbour receives in a
> whole year of toil?[17]

This sort of language was commonplace on the platforms of obscure
Radicals and Socialists but it had never before been heard from a senior

figure in the Cabinet, the inner sanctum of British political life. The effect was electric. Lloyd George was established as the most controversial figure, and possibly the best-known, in politics. In political cartoons and music-hall songs he gained a prominence unknown since the great days of Joseph Chamberlain in the 1890s and early 1900s. To Conservatives he became the devil incarnate, a sort of irresponsible demagogue who debased political life and threatened all the institutions they held dear. But to Liberals in the country he appeared as the party's standard-bearer and a figure who eclipsed even Asquith in many minds. Lloyd George was careful to burnish this reputation by ensuring he received plenty of press coverage. He cultivated notably close relations with many of the major Liberal newspaper editors and owners. Massingham and J. H. Dalziel of *Reynolds News* were old friends. But they were joined after 1906 by Robertson Nicoll of the *British Weekly*, C. P. Scott of the *Manchester Guardian* and Lloyd George's regular golfing partners, George Riddell of the *News of the World* and Robert Donald of the *Daily Chronicle*.[18]

The furore that surrounded Lloyd George in 1909 may have confirmed his public status but it did not make him popular with many of his colleagues, who regarded him with a mixture of envy, distaste for his demagoguery and links with the press and, in the case of younger men like Walter Runciman and Reginald McKenna, rivalry. Essentially he was an isolated figure in the Cabinet once he had broken with his old Radical allies over the Budget. He continued to depend heavily on the Prime Minister for support and his only real friend in the Cabinet was Churchill. When Lloyd Georgian acolytes did gain promotion, like Isaacs in 1912 and Masterman in 1914, they invariably proved failures. Lloyd George might have been the government's second figure in the public's estimation by 1909, but he would have had few supporters in the Cabinet as Asquith's successor. That mantle was always more likely to descend on a less controversial figure like Sir Edward Grey, or even Lord Crewe.[19]

Nevertheless, Lloyd George had made all the running in determining the Liberal Party's strategy in 1908–9. His speeches at Limehouse and Newcastle were not mere expressions of spleen or ambition. They were designed to ensure that the House of Lords was placed in an impossible position. If they swallowed the Budget they could not present this as anything other than a humiliating defeat. But if they rejected it they would have to face a dissolution of Parliament and an election fought on the Lords' powers. In such an election it would be hard for them to pose as champions of the constitution as the Lords had not rejected a Budget in 200 years. In fact, the Lords had little option but to take the second course if they wanted to preserve their authority and the Tory leadership could only follow. On 30 November 1909 the Lords rejected the Budget by 350 votes to 75 and Asquith called a General Election. The result was a narrow victory for the Liberals in January 1910. They lost their overall majority of 1906, but with the likely backing of the infant Labour Party and the Irish Nationalists they could continue in office, even though they only had the same number of seats as the Conservatives.

This was a distinct improvement over anything the Liberals could have hoped for in 1908 and the first time they had won two elections in a row since 1885. Much of the credit had to go to Lloyd George, even though many of his colleagues pointed out the loss of moderate support from 1906.[20] This was probably unavoidable, though, and, to be fair to Lloyd George, he did all he could to keep middle-class Liberals' support. His Budget did not increase taxes for those on modest incomes and his rhetoric was aimed at landowners, not businessmen. Indeed the latter received much praise as fellow-victims of landowners' rapacity. This strategy was partially successful, at least, for the Liberals did retain much middle-class support outside south-eastern England and this was a creditable feat when the party's working-class support had remained so solid.[21]

The government's position in 1910 was not easy, though, and the Cabinet was rent with arguments over ways and means to change the Lords' powers and composition. Then, when it seemed the Cabinet had agreed, at Lloyd George's urging, to demand a guarantee from Edward VII that he would threaten to swamp the Lords with new peers if they would not agree to end their legislative veto, the King died and Tories and Liberals felt they could not refuse to try and negotiate a settlement of the Lords' powers to spare the new King a constitutional crisis. A team of four Tories and four Liberals met until November 1910 in fruitless talks. Lloyd George was one of the Liberal group of four, but otherwise 1910 was a much less exciting year for him. In public he continued to appear a Liberal extremist who was determined to end the Lords' veto. But in private, matters were becoming more complicated.

In the 1910 negotiations Lloyd George showed a willingness to explore compromise that surprised many of his enemies but which he had shown before when the occasion demanded it, notably over the Welsh education revolt.[22] But Lloyd George went much further than this by proposing a programme of agreed action between the parties in two lengthy memoranda.[23] It is very difficult to be sure what he intended, though his actions may well show his impatience with some of his less imaginative colleagues and a sense of his own centrality to British politics. He had solved the financial crisis of 1909 by coming to the problem with an open mind and discarding some old party shibboleths. Perhaps he felt he could also solve most of the outstanding political problems of the day. The coalition proposals were the first real sign that Lloyd George thought his talents should not necessarily be constrained within the existing party system, and when the proposals started to leak out in 1911 this only increased the distrust in which he was held by many senior Liberals. But he may not have seriously expected his coalition proposals to be taken up, nor indeed that the party system was obsolete – there was plenty of partisan invective from Lloyd George after 1910. The key, as Bentley Gilbert has suggested, may well lie in Lloyd George's new National Insurance scheme.[24] The Chancellor's ideas were bound to be controversial, especially with existing insurance interests. If he could secure cross-party support, they stood a much better chance of success.

However, party politics resumed their normal course in November 1910, without agreement. George V insisted on a second election, held in December 1910, which merely duplicated January's result, before he would agree to threaten a mass creation of peers. With this threat hanging over their heads, the Lords agreed to replace their veto with a two-year suspensory power in August 1911. This was a supreme triumph for the Liberals, and Lloyd George in particular, but his fertile mind had already moved on. For him, 1911 was mainly devoted to National Insurance.[25] The origins of this project lay back in 1908, when the Chancellor's attentions had been forcibly directed towards social questions. This was partly because of his close involvement with old age pensions, inherited from Asquith. The huge cost of non-contributory pensions led Lloyd George to take an interest in different methods of financing future social reform. The insurance principle, combining contributions from individuals, their employers and the state, was his solution. This had more than a purely theoretical importance in 1908. Not only was the government deeply unpopular, but trade was depressed and unemployment and poverty generally were central political topics. The Conservatives claimed tariff reform would solve these problems, while Labour proposed greater intervention by the state to provide work for the unemployed. The Liberal government was under pressure to provide its own response. Hence the interest of the Cabinet's two most dynamic figures, Lloyd George and Churchill, in producing answers. They were not alone in their wish to stretch the tenets of Liberalism to include social reform.

By the early 1900s this view was being powerfully propagandised by the
group of journalists, academics and aspirant politicians centred on the
Daily News and the weekly *Nation*.[26] A number of them entered Parliament in the 1906 Liberal landslide, notably C. F. G. Masterman, who
became an intimate of Lloyd George's when he helped him prepare the
1909 Budget. But the 'New Liberals' did not produce specific ideas about
how to develop the state's role in welfare. Rather, they helped to create a
climate of opinion and showed how Liberal language and ideology could
be extended to incorporate state intervention.

These developments helped make Lloyd George's new initiative possible, but the immediate impulse was severely practical and the direction
was highly original. He evolved the concept of health insurance directly
out of his concern at the cost and inadequacy of the 1908 pensions
scheme, while Churchill at the Board of Trade provided the impetus for
an initiative on unemployment. Neither scheme had been widely can-
vassed before 1908. The influence of German precedents can also be
exaggerated – the original ideas in 1908 were obviously based around the
existing systems of private insurance in Britain and Lloyd George seems
to have absorbed little from his famous visit to Germany that year. Nevertheless, matters did not progress much beyond producing some sketches
in 1908. Lloyd George was naturally distracted by the demands of the
1909 Budget and his project only re-emerged in 1910–11. Ironically by
then it was no longer a political imperative. Trade had improved and
constitutional reform rather than poverty dominated the political agenda.
Tariff reform was defeated in 1910 and the Tories were in some dis-
array over its place in their programme. Similarly, Labour had not made
much headway against the Liberals at the two General Elections and
seemed much less threatening than in 1907–8. The whole matter could
have been allowed to drop. It is a measure of Lloyd George's new-found
commitment to welfare reform that he refused to allow this to happen.
His involvement with pensions in 1908 had convinced him that the state
could tackle poverty and the People's Budget had shown how this could
be financed. The elections of 1910 revealed social reform could be an
essential ingredient in Liberal success at the polls, if it was presented with
suitable political skill, and Lloyd George determined to press on and
irrevocably associate Liberalism with further welfare schemes.

National Insurance was always Lloyd George's pet project and one
with which he was inextricably identified in the public mind. Innumerable
cartoons and postcards coupled him with the new National Insurance
stamps with which employers and employees had to familiarise themselves.

It was also one of his greatest achievements, revealing all his superb powers as a negotiator and innovative statesman at their height. Lloyd George took all the initiatives to start the scheme, but he knew himself too well to believe he had the temperament to work out the details. This was left to a hand-picked group of civil servants, working directly to the Chancellor. W. J. Braithwaite has left an impressive picture of their trials and tribulations under their erratic master as they struggled to develop a new system of health care.[27] Freed from the constraints of orthodox departmental work, Lloyd George developed his unusual methods of conducting business even further, as harassed officials chased him for decisions on crucial matters to such unlikely venues as the pier at Nice and the Albion Hotel at Brighton. But in the end he always managed to salvage National Insurance from the difficulties that beset it, particularly the hostility of the British Medical Association and the existing insurance companies. The latter were finally won over by inviting them all to become the bodies that administered the scheme. Everyone in work earning under £160 a year (the working class) was compelled to join an insurance society of some sort and pay weekly contributions towards their health care. This money was topped up by their employers and the state and in return they received sick pay for a specified number of weeks per year, plus the right to consult a doctor contracted to the insurance society. The BMA was outmanoeuvred by the offer of fairly generous salary scales that appealed strongly to the more impoverished doctors. Later in 1913, an experimental scheme of unemployment insurance was developed to cover over two million workers in trades liable to short periods of unemployment.

National Insurance was obviously a limited scheme, but it greatly extended the principle first established in pensions legislation that people should receive state benefits as a right. The state intruded into people's lives in a new and unforeseen way, even if it was through the medium of the insurance companies. The insurance principle was established for social welfare, providing a platform that was to be vastly extended after 1918 and eventually grow into the mid-twentieth century welfare state. Above all, pensions did not stand as an isolated achievement by pre-war Liberals in the field of welfare. It should be emphasised that there was no pressing imperative for the Liberal government to produce more social reform in 1911. It was Lloyd George who conjured up the National Insurance idea and navigated it through the rocky waters of sectional intrigue and national indifference. If anything deserves to secure his long-term reputation as a constructive statesman it is this achievement.

Ironically, if National Insurance helped to secure Lloyd George's reputation for posterity, making him one of the founding-fathers of the welfare state, it marked the start of a troubled period in his short-term political career. While the People's Budget had shown Lloyd George's sure appreciation of what would be popular, National Insurance marked a serious miscalculation of the public mood. An economic boom meant its value as a safety-net was less immediately apparent. It did not, unlike the People's Budget, tax landlords and plutocrats, but ordinary voters. Many small employers, often committed Liberals, heartily disliked the bureaucracy and expense of making National Insurance contributions for each employee, even domestic servants. Nothing the Liberal government did before 1914 caused so much unease among its middle-class constituency. Moreover, this was not compensated for by any upsurge of working-class support. National Insurance was the first tax most working people had to pay to central government and it was correspondingly resented, especially at a time of rising prices when wage rates were under pressure. As a flat-rate tax it bore most heavily on the poorest and the government's bad run of by-election results continued into 1913, the year in which contributions began, with disheartening losses at Newmarket, Reading and South Lanarkshire. This was, to say the least, disappointing news for Lloyd George. The government was committed to repay its debt to the Irish in 1912–14 by introducing a Home Rule Bill and forcing it past the Lords' two-year delaying power. This would undoubtedly dominate political debate and he hoped his new social reform would provide a popular counterweight to a measure that bored most of the electorate and alienated others. Instead he had made a serious miscalculation and his enemies and rivals were keen to point this out.[28] His political stock, that had ridden so high in 1909–10, started to fall.

At the same time, Lloyd George embarked on a number of other dangerous ventures. Not the least of these was his affair with a young woman called Frances Stevenson, who became his secretary in 1912 and his mistress until they married in 1943, after his wife's death. One of the most enduring popular concepts about Lloyd George is that he was an inveterate womaniser and this idea mostly seems to derive from the knowledge in political circles, and much later among the general public, that he had a mistress for most of his married life. The truth is rather more complex. Whatever sexual adventures Lloyd George had as a youth in North Wales are now buried in the mists of time and subsequent rumour. The only public scandal attaching to the early period of Lloyd George's married life was the Edwards divorce case of 1896. Still, it seems likely that he was in fact entirely innocent of any involvement with Mrs Edwards and many subsequent rumours about his sexual adventures once he achieved fame in the 1900s seem to have actually been rehashings of the Edwards case.[29]

Even so, there was a problem in Lloyd George's marriage. His wife, Margaret, was fully aware when they married that he intended to pursue a political career. She, though, had no wish to leave North Wales and her husband did not have the money to provide a suitable house in London for her, and what was to grow into a family of five children, until 1899. He began to look for solace elsewhere and became particularly close to the wives of two other Liberal MPs, 'Mrs Tim' Davies and Julia Henry, and probably had affairs with both of them.[30] His motive seems to have been more a desire for the comforts of home whilst in London and a companion to share his obsession with Westminster politics, rather than an uncontrollable sexual appetite. Rumours about subsequent liaisons after Lloyd George met Frances Stevenson depend on distinctly unreliable sources.[31] In Frances he was provided with a companion who was genuinely absorbed by his political life, in which she was eager and competent to play a full role. She also gave him the unstinting praise that he required. His relationship with Frances scarcely constitutes a record of uncontrolled philandering and it is certainly a slender base for the exotic rumours that grew up about Lloyd George's love life. And yet it was behaviour that was politically dangerous, especially for someone as controversial as Lloyd George, and knowledge about Frances Stevenson's role was tightly guarded, even in political circles, at least until Lloyd George became Minister for Munitions in 1915.

More serious for Lloyd George's public reputation was the Marconi scandal of 1912–13.[32] This has passed into history as one of the great ministerial scandals of the twentieth century and as evidence of Lloyd George's corrupt dealings in public life. The truth is rather less dramatic. Lloyd George had long dabbled in the stock market and continued to do so as Chancellor of the Exchequer (Gladstone and Asquith had done the same). Essentially, he lived in hope of a windfall to alleviate the constant money worries that forced him to rely on the generosity of friends to maintain a ministerial lifestyle. In the past he had been involved in a variety of harebrained schemes, including a gold mine in Patagonia, an insurance company and plans for various newspapers.[33] Then, in April 1912, Godfrey Isaacs, brother of Lloyd George's friend and ally, the Attorney-General, Sir Rufus Isaacs, offered both Ministers the chance to buy into a new stock issue in the American Marconi company, of which he was managing director. He let them know this was likely to yield a quick profit as the company was in the process of buying out its only rivals in the USA. Lloyd George and Rufus Isaacs accepted the offer, though Lloyd George eventually contrived to make a loss on his transactions. To say the least, both men acted extremely foolishly, as the separate English Marconi company had signed a large government contract only the month before. This was public knowledge, so they did not use information gained from their position as ministers to try and make a profit. But they had tried to benefit from inside information about the American stock, whose price may well have been manipulated to an artificial high by Marconi's American directors. Their behaviour was bound to look extremely suspicious if it became public knowledge, especially as the English Marconi contract was widely criticised as unfavourable to the government and leading to speculation in the English company's shares.

This sort of activity was especially dangerous for Lloyd George, who was, after all, the Chancellor of the Exchequer. He had made his Parliamentary reputation in the 1890s by personal attacks on Tory politicians like Joseph Chamberlain and Henry Chaplin, in which he accused them of lining their pockets at the public's expense. Marconi left him open to charges of hypocrisy on which vengeful Tories would be eager to capitalise. The affair fitted neatly into the opposition's strategy of charging the whole government with corruption and the debasement of public life throughout the 1910–14 period. They were accused of selling peerages, bribing the electorate with promises of material rewards and staffing the expanding bureaucracy with Liberal placemen.[34]

Lloyd George and Isaacs attempted to nip any potential scandal in the bud when the Commons debated referring the English Marconi company's contract to a select committee on 11 October 1912. They denied they had ever bought any shares in the English company – which was true, but not the whole truth. But rumours persisted and Isaacs and Lloyd George thought it better to admit their purchase of American Marconi stock in a successful libel action against the *Matin* newspaper in March 1913. Then, in June 1913, the affair took a bizarre turn when it emerged that Alick Murray, the Liberal Chief Whip, had also bought American Marconi stock on behalf of the Liberal Party. The Tories realised, for the first time, that they had a fully-blown political scandal on their hands. The select committee on the Marconi contract split on party lines over the Ministers' behaviour and Lloyd George and Isaacs were only saved by Asquith's robust defence of them in the Commons debate on 18–19 June 1913.

The result was a further fall in Lloyd George's standing with his colleagues. Asquith felt he had to stand by Lloyd George, but this only increased the latter's dependence on the Prime Minister. The Tories were even more bitter against their chief foe, as they felt they had exposed him as a liar and a hypocrite. But the effect on Lloyd George's public reputation is harder to fathom. The Marconi affair was only briefly centre-stage in politics in May–June 1913. Its details were difficult to comprehend and Lloyd George had not actually made any money out of his share deals. As always with political scandals, the impact in Westminster was far greater than that in the country. Fortunately for Lloyd George, politics was also in a particularly partisan phase. Whilst his enemies were only too ready to believe the worst of him, committed Liberals eagerly interpreted the whole affair as a plot against their hero. The scandal did not reveal that Lloyd George was corrupt. But it did show he had little regard for caution or the rules of conventional political morality in his personal life. To many of his opponents, this fitted neatly with his conduct of public office to produce a complete picture of an unscrupulous and untrustworthy politician.

Despite these flirtations with danger, Lloyd George still remained a major force in the Cabinet. He was, for instance, more than ever, the uncrowned king of Welsh politics. When Irish Home Rule was introduced in 1912, to start its two-year battle to overcome the Lords' suspensory veto, it was accompanied by a Bill to disestablish the Welsh Church, possibly in an attempt to appease Nonconformist opinion. At last this measure could now pass the Lords, too, and Lloyd George revelled in his role of champion of the Welsh people against Anglican privilege when introducing the Bill.[35] His grip tightened in other ways, too. Lloyd George's Welsh allies like Ellis Griffiths, Herbert Lewis and William Jones began to climb the lower rungs of government office and the establishment of the Welsh section of the National Insurance administration provided another rich source of patronage. Lloyd George's view of himself as the unofficial leader of his people was embodied in his role in initiating and presiding over, as Constable of Caernarvon Castle, the instalment of the new heir to the throne as Prince of Wales in 1911.[36] His prestige in Wales was never higher than this period between his arrival in high office in 1908 and the 1918 election. A Welsh Liberal journalist commented on 'the editorial dread of saying anything which may be construed into an attack or reflection on the new St David'.[37] But his role in Wales was based on the awe his countrymen felt for his achievements and abilities. He still did not control the local Liberal parties and his influence in South Wales remained much weaker than in the North. In particular, he had no special influence on the industrial disputes of South Wales among miners or mine-owners, as the 1912 coal strike showed.

The problems Lloyd George encountered with National Insurance and the Marconi scandal did not prevent him from continuing to play a central role in the Cabinet's decision-making. But he did not have a decisive affect on the Irish Home Rule crisis facing the Cabinet. Lloyd George, like many Welshmen, had a highly ambiguous attitude to Home Rule and the Irish. While officially committed to Home Rule, he was, naturally enough, keen to pay attention to the national aspirations of the other non-English nations in the United Kingdom, and he included the Protestants of Ulster in this category. With Churchill, he argued with increasing force in 1912–13 that some concessions would have to be made to Ulster.[38] Asquith did not necessarily disagree with this thinking, but he did not feel the Irish Nationalist leader, John Redmond, could persuade his followers to make any concessions until they were convinced that the alternative was civil war in Ireland. This meant waiting until 1914, rather than including terms for Ulster in the intitial Home Rule Bill introduced in 1912. But Bonar Law's strategy ensured the Liberals had to persuade Redmond to compromise. Increasingly, the Tory case against Home Rule focused on the injustices of forcing rule from Dublin onto Ulster. Only by making concessions could the Liberals cut the ground from under Bonar Law's feet. However, this remained very much Asquith's territory and Lloyd George did no more than provide powerful backing for his chief, especially in presenting the case for excluding Ulster to the Nationalists in March 1914.

Despite his role in trying to find a solution to the Cabinet's Irish difficulties, Lloyd George had seemed a much less creative and constructive figure since 1911 and so had the government. Its performance at by-elections nose-dived in 1912 and its main policies of Irish Home Rule and Welsh Church disestablishment meant little to most voters. It is not surprising that in 1912 Lloyd George's mind started to turn to devising ways out of this situation (and reviving his own prestige in the government). Nor is it surprising that he returned to the land issue, the fulcrum of his triumphant strategy in 1909–10. But, Lloyd George did not propose merely to rehash the policies of the People's Budget and the constitutional crisis it provoked. Instead, he intended to develop a carefully planned strategy to unite the party, increase its commitment to social reform while avoiding the unpopularity of National Insurance, discomfit its opponents and correct its underperformance in English rural seats.

Lloyd George delegated the formulation of this new plan to an elaborate Land Enquiry, effectively headed by the social investigator, Seebohm Rowntree.[39] Lloyd George had already used a small band of advisers and experts to help him develop the People's Budget and the National Insurance scheme. The Land Enquiry represented a further extension of a method he was to favour all his life. But it was also an innovation. Lloyd George was suggesting that, for the first time, his party should put a detailed programme of action to the country at an election. He intended that the next Liberal government should not just respond to events, but follow a definite strategy, reflecting his own increased confidence in the role of government in society.

The Enquiry produced two weighty Land Reports, on Rural Land in October 1913 and Urban Land in April 1914. The Rural Report proposed that the Liberals should centre their appeal to the English countryside on a minimum wage for agricultural labourers, with farmers being compensated by security of tenure and rent courts. The Urban Report was much more complex, but it essentially recommended a huge increase in local authorities' role in the housing market, with widespread land purchase and an urban minimum wage as well. These bold measures of social reform were bound together under the banner of the 'land issue', because the reports claimed it was landowners who were to blame for the country's social problems – it was they who had depressed living standards and tyrannised the countryside and they who charged extortionate prices for land, thus producing overcrowding, high rents and slum conditions in the towns. This focus on the landed enemy would hopefully reconcile more cautious Liberals to a further large instalment of social reform, while again outflanking Labour and forcing the Conservatives onto the defensive about their links with landlordism.

Using the land issue in this way was clearly not an irrelevant piece of arcadianism. It was a political strategy very much rooted in the contemporary political circumstances of Edwardian Britain, and it helped to revive Lloyd George's standing in the party before 1914. He presented the rural conclusions of his Enquiry to the Cabinet in October 1913 and they were accepted without any difficulty as the basis of the party's appeal to the country at the next election.[40] The Land Campaign was launched by Lloyd George on 11 October at Bedford and the available evidence suggests that it greatly improved Liberal prospects at the next General Election in English agricultural seats. In a close election, which by-elections indicated by 1914, this advantage in rural England, combined with Liberal plans to abolish plural voting, could have turned the result in the Liberals' favour.[41] Moreover, the Cabinet's, and the party's, willing acceptance of Lloyd George's plans showed he was still the man who was expected to determine the main outlines of the party's direction. He was the party's greatest creative force and he was by no means exhausted by nearly nine years in office.

In many ways, though, the most intriguing aspect of the Land Campaign was its urban element, for this promised to take the party into new areas of social reform. Unfortunately for historians, these proposals were only approved by the Cabinet shortly before war broke out in August 1914, and so had little impact in the country, but they indicate very strongly the interventionist direction in which Lloyd George proposed to lead his party. Most Liberals were willing to accept further social reform if it was packaged, in the manner of the Land Campaign, as an assault on privilege and Lloyd George showed no sign of allowing the pace to slacken. His 1914 Budget pushed on from 1909, by raising more direct taxes on the very wealthy to finance future reforms.[42] Although this project ran into some difficulties with the Parliamentary timetable, the party stood on the brink of further efforts to expand the embryo welfare state when war intervened and diverted Lloyd George and Liberalism into very different paths.

Foreign policy did not take up much of Lloyd George's time before 1914. The Boer War had associated him with the Radical wing of the Liberal Party, but, as we have seen, Lloyd George was a critic of that war because he wished to embarrass the Tory government, rather than out of principle. He had certainly been a great disappointment to the Radicals as Chancellor of the Exchequer. In particular, he had not proved a great economiser of naval expenditure in any of the Cabinet crises in 1908–9, 1911–12 and 1913–14. Unknown to all but a few Cabinet colleagues, he had also approved the government's increasing links with the French armed forces from 1911 onwards, including the implicit commitment to defend France from German attack.[43] It was not, therefore, inconsistent for Lloyd George to approve the decision to go to war in 1914, even before the invasion of Belgium swung most Liberals behind the idea. The most notable fact about Lloyd George's behaviour during the crisis of July–August 1914 was that he said and did so little. By refusing to lead a Radical campaign against war, he greatly enhanced Asquith's chances of leading a united Cabinet into the conflict.

Lloyd George's attitude to foreign policy can be viewed from a number of angles. It can partly be explained as a necessary consequence of his domestic strategy. While he did try to restrain naval spending during his time as Chancellor, it was not a position he was prepared to put before all else. He would have had to sacrifice his whole domestic programme if he had resigned or contributed to the break-up of the Cabinet over naval spending. Moreover, his own fiscal strategy after 1908 ensured he never really had to face a straight choice between expenditure on arms and social reform. His soaking of the very rich through graduated direct taxation meant he could do both. Primarily in 1908–14, he was a social reformer who needed a united Liberal Cabinet to carry out his plans. Once again in August 1914, Cabinet unity was his primary aim. He probably hoped that, with luck, the war would be over quickly, Liberalism's popularity would be boosted and the electorate could then turn to his Land Campaign. But if he led a non-interventionist crusade, the Cabinet would split and the most likely outcome would be a Liberal Imperialist–Conservative coalition to pursue the war. Moreover, as he told C. P. Scott, a campaign in the country against a war in 1914 could not be as effective as their anti-Boer War activities. That had been an imperial sideshow. In 1914, most British people would see that 'the stakes were too great' for the country and war was necessary for national survival.[44]

But this does not entirely explain Lloyd George's acceptance of the need to make military commitments to France as early as 1911 and his own occasional belligerence, as in his Mansion House speech of August 1911. In private, he went even further, several times mentioning to colleagues his enthusiasm for some form of national service or conscription.[45] This attitude of Lloyd George's was not due to overweening francophilia or germanophobia. As Ken Morgan has pointed out, Lloyd George held highly ambivalent views about both countries.[46] Rather, it makes more sense to see his attitudes as the counterpart, in foreign and defence policy, of his discovery of the power of the state to transform people's lives through social welfare. If a strong state could end poverty it could also maintain Britain's role in the world and require sacrifices from its citizens.

This does not make Lloyd George a war-monger. No doubt he could justify the French commitment to himself on the grounds that it would preserve peace by deterring German expansionism. There were many Liberal versions of what a 'truly' Liberal foreign policy might be, apart from the Little Englandism of some of the Radicals. Liberals disliked aggression and the abrogation of treaties quite as much as entangling foreign alliances. However, in August 1914, Lloyd George refused to back a 'peace at any price' strategy. As ever, when attacked he never favoured retreat. He did not know what such a war would entail, but then nobody did in 1914. What was clear, though, was that he had come a long way from the uncomplicated Radical people had known in 1905. In fact, his combination of social reform and a robust foreign policy had brought him very close to the position of Liberal Imperialists like Asquith, Haldane and Winston Churchill. Where he differed from them was in his continued identification with Radical causes like Welsh Church disestablishment and attacks on landlords. This unique combination of Radical and Imperialist sympathies made Lloyd George a rather isolated figure in the Cabinet, but, as August 1914 demonstrated, he was in a pivotal position. His inaction deprived the Radicals of a leader and smoothed Britain's entry into the war.

3
WAR, 1914–18

The old myth that Britain was unprepared for war in 1914 has long been exploded.[1] The Army actually had a good idea of the kind of war Britain should fight against a German invasion of France. The British Expeditionary Force would provide some limited aid to the French in defending their eastern frontier. Meanwhile, the Navy would strangle German overseas trade and destroy the German fleet in a great naval battle in the North Sea. Britain would thus be able to destroy Germany and restore a balance of power in Europe in a short war with minimal damage to her economy and trade. This was a perfectly reasonable assessment of the likely outcome of events in the summer of 1914. If it had proved correct the Liberal Party would have emerged unscathed from the conflict and Lloyd George's career would probably have remained within the bounds of the existing party system. Unfortunately for the Liberal Party, the experts' predictions proved totally inaccurate. No decisive battle was fought on either the Western or Eastern Front and the war settled down to the stalemate of the trenches. By the time the war ended in 1918, over five million British men were in the armed forces, more than 700 000 had been killed and the economy had suffered massive dislocation. But there was no revolution, remarkably little disaffection and a huge upsurge of patriotism. Under the strain, though, the pre-war political system broke asunder, destroying parties and forging new and strange alliances. The ultimate beneficiary of this was Lloyd George, who gained the premiership, something he could not have expected before 1914.

But none of this was immediately apparent in August 1914. Instead, Lloyd George was thrust into the unfamiliar world of banks and interest rates. He had never given much attention to such matters before, when he was Chancellor. Charles Hobhouse claimed the whole field was

'Greek to him'.[2] Indeed, Lloyd George's habit of undertaking huge schemes, like National Insurance, outside the area of his office meant he had never been more than a part-time Chancellor. Details were always left to somebody else. But in August 1914 he was faced with the need to calm a possible financial panic that could have destroyed Britain's war effort before it even began. As ever, Lloyd George proved remarkably quick to learn from any helpful source, even importing Austen Chamberlain from the opposition benches to help out in negotiations. He took the right advice to restore confidence and acted on it promptly, raising interest rates, closing the banks for three days, authorising the issue of paper money, guaranteeing export credits and enforcing a moratorium on bills for three months.[3] The incipient panic passed, leaving Lloyd George's standing at an improbable high in the City, if only because his actions had given the bankers everything they wanted. Doubts about his ability to handle the nation's finances were swept away and even his bitterest foes in the Cabinet were impressed.

Most of this was, of course, unknown to the public. To many Conservatives and even uncommitted observers, Lloyd George was still publicly identified with the Radical section of the Cabinet who had opposed arms expenditure and foreign alliances before 1914 and who were thought to have been reluctant to declare war and, possibly, unenthusiastic about prosecuting the conflict. In the Cabinet, of course, it had long been clear that Lloyd George was no longer an ally of the Radicals. But, in the mood of overwhelming patriotism prevalent in 1914, this point had to be made in public if Lloyd George was to gain from the new political situation the war had brought. He set out to do this in a widely publicised speech at the Queen's Hall on 17 September 1914. In it he called on the British people to rally to the war as a great moral crusade. There was an overwhelmingly favourable response, establishing him at once in the public mind as someone who stood for a wholehearted conduct of the war. Over two and a half million copies of the speech were distributed and Sir Edward Grey claimed to have been moved to tears by its noble sentiments.[4] Lloyd George became the first and foremost of the Liberal leaders to tap into popular patriotism and to reach out beyond his party to the whole country. In war, just as in peace, he very quickly seemed indispensable, however much old enmities continued to smoulder in the Cabinet. Before 1914, Lloyd George's oratorical fireworks had divided him from his Conservative opponents. By taking up a vigorously pro-war position he slowly started to build bridges across the political divide in ways that were ultimately to prove crucial in his ascent to the premiership.

In the Cabinet, Lloyd George continued his pre-war practice of fulfilling a number of different roles. He had no intention of being pigeon-holed purely as a Chancellor, just because he had shown in August 1914 that he could master the technical side of the job. He certainly had no intention of being excluded from the crucial decisions about the running of the war. For the moment, Lloyd George the social reformer was left behind. Once different daily priorities faced the Chancellor, a new political figure arose – Lloyd George the war leader. This transformation was made rather easier because, as one of the Cabinet's leading figures, he was always included in the smaller committees that Asquith set up to deal with the multifarious problems and decisions involved in conducting a war. The Cabinet itself was too swamped with work and buffeted in too many directions by the different priorities of its members to deal with the new workload. The detailed conduct of the war was devolved to a succession of committees – first the War Council, then the Dardanelles committee and finally the War committee.[5] All these groups suffered the same fate. Gradually they grew in size and were overwhelmed by details, forcing the creation of a new committee.

Lloyd George's war strategy became apparent remarkably early in the discussions in these committees. Essentially, it did not change throughout the war. First, he consistently urged that the ultimate control of military strategy should be in the hands of politicians, not soldiers. His motto was a saying he attributed to Briand, 'This war is too important to be left to military men.'[6] This seemed natural enough to him – after all, he was a politician and one with an amateur interest in strategy. During the Boer War he had followed troop manoeuvres carefully and commented in detail on the various commanders' mistakes.[7] But this was actually an extremely controversial position. Most Conservatives venerated the Army as the embodiment of the nation, something above politics, and hated the thought of 'mere' politicians giving orders to generals. Some Liberals agreed with them. They believed war should be left to professional soldiers, rather than to a politician who might aspire to a sort of military dictatorship. Nevertheless, Lloyd George's self-confidence did not waver and throughout 1914–18 he never ceased to question military advice and to try and vest ultimate control of strategy in the Cabinet.

Lloyd George believed that only politicians could take a wide enough view of the war to determine the broad outlines of military policy. Throughout the conflict he appreciated that it was being fought across Europe and Asia and he was not a consistent advocate of concentrating all military resources on the Western Front. He was unimpressed by his first visit to the trenches in October 1914, telling his wife, 'It is *stalemate*. We cannot turn them out of their trenches and they cannot turn us out.'[8] On 1 January 1915 he subjected his colleagues to a long memorandum arguing for an Allied landing in the Balkans and, later in the war, he was, at various times, to urge action in places as far apart as Italy and Palestine.[9] In his *War Memoirs*, Lloyd George claimed that all of these policies were part of a determined attempt to avoid the slaughter of the trenches and win the war by quicker and more ingenious means. This neatly shifted the responsibility for blood-lettings like the Somme in 1916 and Passchendaele in 1917 onto the military and their 'infatuation of a breakthrough which haunted the western generals like a disease of the mind'.[10] But the truth was much more complicated. Lloyd George only intermittently favoured an 'Eastern' strategy. As War Minister at the time of the Somme and Prime Minister when Passchendaele was launched, he approved these projects as the best way to fight the war in 1916–17. It would be closer to the truth to say that he was constantly casting around for a scheme that would produce victory on the Eastern or Western Fronts.

As David French has persuasively argued, the real conflict in the Cabinet in 1914–16 was not over where the war should be fought but how it should be fought.[11] Lloyd George's most distinctive contribution was in his response to this problem. In August 1914, the Cabinet had been stunned by the announcement by their new War Minister, Lord Kitchener, that he intended to seek volunteers for an Army several million strong and that the war would last at least two or three years. But it soon became clear that Kitchener was undoubtedly correct in his assessment of the situation. Given the stalemate that had developed by October 1914, the French and Russians would never have accepted Britain sending only a token force to fight on the Western Front and a huge British Army would obviously be required to help defeat the German war machine.

But the implications of this commitment were alarming. By December 1914 over one million men were in uniform and by the spring of 1915 nearly a third of the employed male labour force had enlisted or joined a war-related industry.[12] This meant that the assumption that the economy could function more or less as in peace-time – 'business as usual' as Lloyd George called it on 4 August – was rapidly invalidated.[13] The Cabinet was unsure how it should proceed, for all courses of action were fraught with difficulties. Reginald McKenna represented one viewpoint.[14] He feared the country could not feed and equip the huge Army the generals were creating without destroying its economy. Instead, he argued that the size of the Army should be limited to what Britain could afford, while she concentrated on being the economic powerhouse, munitions factory and paymaster of the Alliance. The problem with this approach was that without a huge Army, Britain had no prospect of defeating Germany. At the opposite pole, Kitchener naturally wished to make the creation of his Army the first priority, though he did not initially wish to use it in great offensives until the Germans were exhausted in 1916–17. Unfortunately, this hardly accorded with economic realities. Massive volunteering denuded munitions factories and essential industries of men, reducing production and exports just when they needed a boost to equip and pay for the new Army.

Most of the Cabinet groped around between these two views. Only Lloyd George had the daring and open-mindedness to produce a distinctive response. On 22 February 1915 he circulated another memorandum to his harassed colleagues.[15] In it, he suggested that for victory to be ensured, the Army would have to expand by another one to one and a half million men *and* munitions production would have to massively increase, both to supply the Army and those of Britain's Allies, especially Russia. He was effectively arguing for a simultaneous pursuit of the Kitchener and McKenna strategies – far more than anyone else in the Cabinet thought the country could sustain. The key was munitions, an area Lloyd George had concentrated on increasingly since October 1914. He claimed 'we could double our effective energies if we organised our factories thoroughly. All the engineering works of the country ought to be turned on to the production of war material.' If this could be achieved the circle could be squared and Britain could supply both a huge Army and its Allies. In effect, Lloyd George was arguing for a total commitment to victory from all of society, under the direction of the government. This was to become his message for the entire war.

Lloyd George believed he was the man to deliver the goods. He persuaded Asquith to agree to a new Defence of the Realm Act in March 1915, authorising the government effectively to take over the direction of the engineering industry. This would mean replacing 'business as usual' with 'victory as usual', the Chancellor claimed.[16] Lloyd George then built on his expertise in labour relations at the Board of Trade to negotiate a voluntary agreement with the engineering unions to suspend restrictive practices during the war. On 23 March he took charge of a new committee to mobilise the industry for munitions production. Unfortunately, this involved a head-on collision with Kitchener. The War Minister saw

Lloyd George as an intruder and a rival. Moreover, he wished to concentrate production on existing War Office contractors. This would produce quick results for his armies and build on existing expertise. Lloyd George, on the contrary, wanted a revolutionary increase in production and that could only be achieved by developing new sources of supply. The battle dragged on through April and May 1915, becoming increasingly personal and fraught.

The stance he took had immense implications for Lloyd George, for it allied him unquestionably with most Tories, who wished to put winning the war before all else, though some figures like Arthur Balfour and Lord Lansdowne were worried the strain would ultimately weaken British power. However, it is not clear that Lloyd George had suddenly become more 'right-wing' or abandoned his Liberalism as a result of the war. Most Liberals were eager to win the war as soon as possible and Nonconformity had its martial as well as its pacifist side (very much to the fore in 1914–18). Lloyd George did disagree, though, with Cabinet colleagues like McKenna and Runciman over the degree to which the economy should be controlled to increase war production. Behind this argument there lay instinctively different reactions to the prospect of increasing the state's role in the economy and society. These attitudes pre-dated the war. Lloyd George's enthusiasm for state control in 1915 was, in many ways, a development of his pre-war interest in mobilising the state to fight poverty. Similarly, McKenna and his allies had been lukewarm social reformers and carried their dislike of state control into wartime. In reality, Lloyd George had hardly moved to the 'right' in 1914–15, nor had he ceased to be a Liberal. It is true that he was unconcerned by the potential threat to civil liberties involved in greater state control in wartime. But his argument with Runciman and McKenna was not conducted in those terms. It was a dispute about the best way to win the war, not a matter of essential principles that could not be compromised.[17]

The really telling criticism of Lloyd George in 1914–15 was not that he suddenly became a reactionary, but that he did nothing to put in place a financial base for war. Tax rises were inadequate in both his 1914 emergency war Budget and his 1915 Budget.[18] In 1915, the war was mainly being financed by loans and a foreign exchange crisis was also looming because of huge armaments purchases in the USA. Lloyd George was perhaps too busy trying to *run* the war to give serious attention to devising the financial means to *win* it. Ironically, it was left to his successor at the Treasury, McKenna, who did not share his faith in total war, to make substantial tax increases.

In the long term, though, the Liberal government had more serious problems than Lloyd George's erratic attention to his duties at the Exchequer, for once it became clear that the war would not be over quickly it was unlikely the government could survive without forming a coalition with its Tory opponents. The Conservatives had kept an uneasy truce with the government since the outbreak of war. But backbenchers and the Tory press were increasingly restive at what they interpreted as the government's half-hearted and incompetent conduct of the war, while Bonar Law was anxious to contain any outburst of criticism for fear it would wreck the image of national unity in wartime. Finally, in the spring of 1915, the storm broke. Almost simultaneously, newspaper headlines appeared, inspired by figures in the Army, claiming that British forces were desperately short of shells, and the aged and unpredictable head of the Navy, Lord Fisher, resigned.[19] Bonar Law went to Asquith and told him that he could no longer refrain from criticising the government. They agreed the only way to preserve a semblance of unity among the politicians was to form a coalition.

Lloyd George was happy with this turn of events – indeed he urged a coalition on Asquith and Bonar Law. There is no need to see in this a deeply laid plot. But a coalition obviously fitted in with Lloyd George's idea of a war that would mobilise all of the nation's talent and resources. It also opened up a new political situation. It was unlikely Lloyd George would ever have succeeded Asquith as Liberal leader. He was popular in the party at large but he had too many personal enemies in the Cabinet who regarded him as an unprincipled demagogue. But war changed all this. Once the government was a coalition it was no longer necessary to be Liberal leader to be Prime Minister.

The immediate consequence of May 1915 for Lloyd George, though, was his departure from the Exchequer to the newly created post of Minister for Munitions, with responsibility for increasing production and avoiding any more 'shell scandals'. The embarrassing publicity of May 1915 did not damage Kitchener's public reputation, but it lost him the confidence of his colleagues and his battle with Lloyd George over munitions. Asquith no doubt saw this as a shrewd move on his part. He gave Lloyd George a specific task, rather than seeing him range over the whole of war policy as an unpredictable force, and he made it look as if the Liberals were keen to take action to ensure a vigorous prosecution of the war. However, this was also a high-risk strategy by Asquith. If Lloyd George succeeded, his status in the government and the country would be immeasurably enhanced. Moreover, he would be able to present a different sort of war leadership to the country. In contrast to Asquith's role as chairman of the Cabinet, Lloyd George would be able to offer himself as the dynamic leader and mobiliser of the nation's resources. Asquith was not a dilatory or lazy war leader, but he saw no reason to change his routine of bridge games and lunches with society ladies. But, as Bonar Law said, 'In war it is necessary not only to be active but to seem active', and Asquith often failed in this.[20] Lloyd George, on the other hand, was careful to burnish his image as the dynamic man of action – hence his fury at press reports that he had visited the Latin Quarter whilst attending a conference in Paris in 1915.[21] In many ways, the Asquith–Lloyd George clash was implicit from the moment the latter took over at Munitions.

In fact, Lloyd George's stint as Minister of Munitions in 1915–16 did make his reputation as a war leader. The image that Lloyd George created around this time at munitions has even survived the attentions of revisionist historians.[22] Essentially, it did make sense to hive munitions production off from the War Office – the task had simply become too big. Moreover, Lloyd George's role there was ideally suited to his talents. Rather than being faced with a huge bureaucracy, he was able to create his own organisation more or less from scratch. He was able to exercise his talent for picking the right person for the job on a huge scale (though his subordinate, Christopher Addison, deserves some of the credit, too). The famous men of 'push and go' were recruited from industry to work alongside civil servants, academics and anyone else the Minister felt would be useful. This meant in turn, Lloyd George did not have to undertake any detailed administration, never his strong point, confident that he had competent subordinates. The flexibility of the new Ministry also meant it could both accommodate Lloyd George's sudden enthusiasms for new projects and it could be personally motivated by the Minister's extraordinary personality. The system had its weaknesses, of course. Most of the appointees had little in the way of defined responsibilities and had to engage in a war against their alleged colleagues to build their own empire. There was no appeal except to Lloyd George personally and his decisions were often capricious. Gradually, the Ministry of Munitions became like any other Whitehall department, but before this happened its task had already been completed.

The yardstick by which the Ministry was judged was its ability to increase production and in this it was largely successful. Lloyd George took full advantage of a new Munitions of War Act in July 1915 to establish the industry's priority in commandeering fuel, transport, land, raw materials and imports. Not only did the Ministry raise the targets for munitions production, it took steps itself to raise capacity, speed up production by eliminating inefficiencies in the manufacturing process and make technical innovations. It set up state factories to produce munitions, organised existing factories into regional groups of producers, told them what to produce and pursued vital research into the development of shells and machine guns. As Lloyd George boasted in his *War Memoirs*, Britain produced 70 000 filled shells per week in May 1915 and 238 000 per week by January 1916.[23] Undeniably, munitions production soared, but it was not enough to meet Lloyd George's grand vision in February 1915. At the same time, in 1915–16, the British line on the Western Front had increased from 36 to 85 miles and British divisions had risen from 14 to 42.[24] Lloyd George's achievement allowed Britain to go on fighting, rather than giving it a decisive chance of winning.

This success at Munitions, however, raised other questions that were far more difficult to answer. The most significant of these focused on how the nation's manpower should best be directed to win the war. The Army's demand for more men was insatiable and it was increasingly clear during 1915 that voluntary recruiting could not keep pace with demand. Moreover, the Army was in competition for men who were desperately needed in the factories and on the land, as Lloyd George had painfully discovered at Munitions. He regarded conscription as the only possible solution to these difficulties. To him, this was merely the logical extension of his experiments with state control at the Ministry of Munitions. By September 1915, his position on conscription was public knowledge.[25] Most Conservatives supported Lloyd George's views, but Liberal and Labour reactions were complicated. Labour hated any thought of industrial conscription and were consequently suspicious of, if not implacably hostile to, conscription into the Army. Lloyd George was the only Liberal in the Cabinet who enthusiastically advocated conscription, though 40 or so backbenchers supported him. Reginald McKenna was, unsurprisingly, conscription's most prominent Liberal opponent. He argued it would be a disaster because the country could not afford an even larger army and, by taking more men from industry, conscription would ruin the economy and prevent the Army, let alone the Allies, being properly supplied. This dispute was clearly a natural development of earlier arguments in 1914–15 about military strategy and the state's role in the economy. Outside the Cabinet, most Liberal MPs were reluctant to accept conscription on a mixture of practical and ideological grounds, but less than 30 backbenchers were implacably opposed to it in principle. If pressed, the rest were prepared to accept conscription as a

necessary price to win the war. Nevertheless, Lloyd George's close association with the cause of conscription finally disillusioned those Liberals
who still believed he was a pre-war Radical. The demands of organising
the wartime economy encouraged him to push Liberals' enthusiasm for
an active state to its limits. Even those who finally agreed with him over
conscription did not always forgive him for straining their loyalties so
severely.

The advocates of conscription won in stages in 1915–16.[26] They had
the united backing of the Conservatives and opposition from Liberals
and Labour that proved increasingly soft. Further, if the British were to
participate in the huge combined Allied offensive proposed for 1916,
they would need conscription to replace their losses in the field. Step by
step the government moved towards finally passing a conscription Bill in
June 1916. This was the last great triumph of Asquithian management.
Asquith saw the inevitability of conscription and used his cautious
approach to the matter to bring with him the vast majority of Liberals. His
handling of the matter was certainly not flawless – he made at least one
uncharacteristic misjudgement of the mood of the Commons – but he
was still in command of his role as the government's chairman and mediator. As Lloyd George said, he was 'the only man who can get Compul-
sion through the *House of Commons* at present'.[27] Ironically, though,
Asquith's great success in preserving his government virtually intact
through the conscription crisis made him much more vulnerable. Once
he had piloted conscription through the Commons his Tory allies needed
him much less. Moreover, his gradual approach allowed the argument to
fester and Lloyd George's patience with his old chief started to wear thin.
'[I]f he were in the pay of the Germans he could not be of more complete
use to them,' Lloyd George complained.[28]

At the same time, in the latter half of 1916, several crises were blowing
up that were eventually to destroy Asquith's premiership and elevate
Lloyd George to the highest office. The background was the increasing
sense of frustration in political circles that victory in the war seemed no
closer. Indeed, Britain's problems seemed to be mounting. The great
Somme offensive did not bring victory, however it was presented. Instead,
it coincided with a major British reverse in the Middle East and the collapse
of Rumania on the Eastern Front. Food production remained desperately
close to the minimum level needed to feed the population and the
manpower question was still not resolved, despite the introduction of
conscription, with the Army, agriculture, industry and transport all
demanding more recruits. Finally, Britain was increasingly dependent

on credit to buy essential war materials in the USA and it was by no means
clear that American bankers would go on lending to Britain.

In the face of these problems a few hearts in the inner circle of politics
started to quail. Lord Lansdowne summed up this mood in a memorandum, discussed by the Cabinet on 22 November 1916, in which he raised
the possibility that Britain should try and make a compromise peace
before its resources were exhausted.[29] Most politicians rejected this course
as impractical and defeatist. But it made Asquith vulnerable to the charge
that he was not providing vigorous enough leadership to combat British
reverses and forestall defeatist talk. This sort of criticism had become
commonplace in the Conservative press and on the backbenches in the
autumn of 1916. Its mouthpiece was Edward Carson, who told anyone
who would listen that the only way to enliven the leadership of the country was to create a small War Cabinet to take the daily decisions necessary
to the conduct of the war. Conservative Ministers felt this dissatisfaction
to varying degrees, but most were unwilling to act on it. Criticism of
Asquith was also, to some degree, criticism of them. Moreover, they were
aware of the difficulties of removing the Prime Minister. If they threatened resignation it would look like unpatriotic desertion of their posts
and they were anxious to retain Labour and the Liberals in the Cabinet to
ensure the country remained united behind the war effort – more essential than ever in the dark days at the end of 1916. But most Liberals, and
possibly Labour as well, would surely not accept the deposition of their
chief.

Therefore, if Asquith was going to be toppled, it had to be by one of his
own party and Lloyd George was the obvious contender as the most
prominent Liberal after the Prime Minister. He was also becoming
increasingly weary of the arguments within the Cabinet. In his *War Memoirs*
he referred to 'the sense of frustration and tangled impotence which
oppressed me during those closing months of 1916'.[30] McKenna and his
allies continued to argue for a husbanding of British resources and
relations with Lloyd George were reaching a new low. Frances Stevenson
called McKenna 'the only person whom D. really detests'.[31] This made
Lloyd George more amenable to some reconstruction of the government, especially one that would bypass the interminable wrangles in
the Cabinet. In November 1916 he started to give the War Cabinet idea
serious consideration. As part of this strategy, Asquith would have to be
removed from effective power, at least over the war, and thus excluded
from the War Cabinet. To include him would merely perpetuate the
existing wrangles and tendency to what Lloyd George saw as drift

and muddle. However, Lloyd George seems to have had no thought of removing him from the premiership. Most Liberals would not accept this and Asquith would be needed to keep McKenna and his allies in line.

There may also have been another factor in Lloyd George's mind. In the spring of 1916 he had left Munitions to succeed Kitchener at the War Office. This was ostensibly a promotion and Lloyd George probably welcomed the idea because he felt his job was done at Munitions and no more could be gained from the post. More importantly, the Army was about to launch its Somme offensive as part of the Allies' co-ordinated attack on all fronts. If it succeeded, Lloyd George could not allow anyone else to claim the credit. But in fact the War Office proved a gilded cage. Lloyd George could not enforce decisions on strategy on the Army, despite his conviction that British generals had 'no ingenuity'.[32] In particular, he could not circumvent the Chief of the Imperial General Staff, Sir William Robertson, who could always appeal to the Cabinet (or even the King) against his Minister. Robertson and Sir Douglas Haig, the commander in France, proved more than a match for Lloyd George in the black arts of politics and scored a number of direct hits on their political chief. In September 1916, for instance, Lloyd George unwisely questioned some French generals about British tactics. This was leaked to the *Morning Post* on 28 September 1916 and Lloyd George found himself pilloried for lack of patriotism. Most crucially, the Somme was a bloody failure and Lloyd George to some extent had to take the blame for this. His political prestige began unavoidably to wane.

The other blow to his political standing had been the aftermath of the Easter Rising in Ireland.[33] Asquith had assigned Lloyd George the task of producing a settlement that would keep Nationalist opinion behind the war, without alienating the Unionists, who had powerful friends in the Conservative ranks. Lloyd George took on the job with some reluctance and after hurried negotiations produced a plan for immediate Home Rule outside a six-county Northern Ireland. It was not clear if this was acceptable to the Nationalists, nor whether they could persuade their followers to accept the plan. Lloyd George practised some sleight of hand by promising John Redmond and Sir Edward Carson different things regarding the permanence of partition. Probably the events of 1916 had already moved most Nationalist opinion beyond the old idea of Home Rule. But the plan fell at the first hurdle because some Conservatives in the Cabinet could not accept the abandonment of the southern Unionists to Home Rule. Lloyd George had tried over Ireland, but he had also

failed and together with his problems at the War Office this meant his
star was no longer in the ascendant in late 1916.

Thus he may also have turned to the War Cabinet scheme in an effort
to reassert both his claims to direct the conduct of the war and his own
position in the Cabinet. But he was careful to co-ordinate his strategy with
Bonar Law, who wished to reconstruct the government, if only to convince his restive backbenchers that the war would be prosecuted more
vigorously. After initial approaches by Bonar Law, Lloyd George wrote
to Asquith on 1 December 1916 outlining a plan for a small War Cabinet
to meet almost daily and take the crucial decisions on the running of the
war.[34] The Prime Minister would be excluded, as would his cronies like
Runciman and McKenna, who had disagreed so violently with Lloyd
George. But Asquith would remain as Prime Minister. Lloyd George
accompanied his War Cabinet proposal by plans for new ministries to pursue more determined action over the looming problems in agricultural
production and manpower. This was meant to be a coherent answer to
Lansdowne's counsel of despair and to show how the war could be won,
thus putting flesh on Lloyd George's call for a 'knock-out blow' against
the Germans. However, this did not become very clear in the ensuing crisis, and much revolved around personalities. Lloyd George made it fairly
apparent that if his proposal was not accepted he would resign. He had
often talked about this in the past, but this time he seems to have been
serious. He may well have calculated that resignation was preferable to
the continuing slide in his reputation at the War Office, while a move to
any other office could only be seen as a demotion.

In fact, there is no great mystery over Lloyd George's motives in the
crisis of 1916. All the controversy surrounds the activities of Asquith and
the Conservative leaders. Asquith's immediate reaction was to negotiate
a settlement. The key to his attitude may have been the impression he
gained from a meeting with Bonar Law that the Tory leaders backed
Lloyd George's plan and that if the War Minister resigned, so would
they, thus bringing the government down. But then Asquith changed his
mind. A number of people have been assigned responsibility for this
course of action, including Reginald and Pamela McKenna, Lord Robert
Cecil and Margot Asquith. Possibly he just came to believe his position
was stronger than he had thought and that he could survive Lloyd
George's resignation, as he had survived those of so many others. Lloyd
George duly resigned and Asquith's confidence started to unravel as it
became clear he did not have the full support of many of the Tory
leaders. Asquith then resigned himself, either in despair or as a final

challenge to his enemies to see if they could form a government without him. Bonar Law declined to try and head a new ministry on the grounds that he could not muster any non-Conservative support. But he suggested George V send for Lloyd George.

This outcome could not have been predicted when the crisis began. Lloyd George had not planned to supplant Asquith as Prime Minister and the latter's downfall was largely the result of the wavering and uncertain intentions of the Tory leadership, under pressure to seem more vigorous in their conduct of the war and uncertain of the need to retain Asquith. If anyone gave Lloyd George his chance in December 1916 it was Bonar Law and it had to be clear to Lloyd George that if he tried to take up the King's offer he would be a Prime Minister dependent on Tory support. Furthermore, he would be splitting the Liberal Party as Asquith would hardly agree to serve under anyone else. Before 1914, Lloyd George had needed a united Liberal Party to carry his schemes for social reform. But once the war gave him new priorities he abandoned his concern for Liberal unity. To Lloyd George all the country's resources had to be mobilised, regardless of party boundaries. In December 1916 he had no hesitation in grabbing the greatest prize in politics.

In a few days of hectic activity, Lloyd George gathered enough support to make good his claim to the premiership. The lure of office was too hard to resist for the Conservative grandees, for with the Asquithian Liberals out of the government virtually all of them achieved better posts. Indeed, the most important party in the new government were obviously the Tories – three of the five members of the new War Cabinet (Law, Lord Curzon and Lord Milner) were Conservatives, for instance. Labour proved remarkably easy to win over, mainly with the promise of more jobs and new Ministries of Labour and Pensions, headed by Labour MPs. Essentially, the Labour MPs and the NEC accepted that it was their patriotic duty to support whatever government was in power, provided it paid attention to working-class demands. In so doing, they finally broke the pre-war bond with the Liberals that had been weakened in May 1915, preparing the way for Labour's emergence as a new political force after 1918.

And yet this momentous event was largely overlooked in 1916. More attention focused on the division in the Liberal ranks. Given the nature of Lloyd George's relations with most of the other Liberal Cabinet Ministers it was not surprising that he did not expect to muster much support from them. Of the ten Liberals in the 1916 Cabinet (excluding Asquith and Lloyd George themselves), the new Prime Minister only offered jobs

to Edwin Montagu and Herbert Samuel. Both refused, though Montagu
relented in 1917 and took the India Office, and Samuel would have liked
to extricate himself from his obligations to his fellow Liberal Ministers.
This distance between Lloyd George and his Liberal colleagues should
not necessarily be seen as an outcome of the war. Most of the other eight
Liberal Ministers were either closely tied to Asquith, like Lord Crewe and
H. J. Tennant (Asquith's brother-in-law), or long-standing enemies of
Lloyd George, like McKenna and Runciman. Lloyd George had been an
outstanding figure in the pre-war Cabinet, but also an isolated one and so
he remained in December 1916. As Lord Selborne put it, 'He had not a
real friend among his Liberal colleagues in the cabinet and most of them
evidently hated him.' [35]

But to form a government he had to demonstrate that he had some
measure of Liberal support outside the leadership. His acolyte, Christopher Addison, produced encouraging lists of Liberal MPs who were said
to be pledged to Lloyd George if he could form a government, but the
ranks of those willing and suitable to hold high office were decidedly
thin.[36] The only Liberal MPs appointed to the wider Cabinet, outside the
War Cabinet, in December 1916 were Sir Frederick Cawley, Christopher
Addison and Robert Munro, none of whom were known to the public
or carried much weight in the party. Their ranks had to be strengthened
by the extra-parliamentary 'experts', Herbert Fisher and D. A. Thomas,
to reach the level of respectability. Lower down the ministerial scale,
though, a clutch of opportunists and committed supporters made themselves known and 26 Liberals were recruited from the Commons, Lords
and outside Parliament to flesh out the idea of a Lloyd George Liberal
following.

The real situation was probably that most Liberals were utterly bewildered by the events of December 1916. They had certainly not been consulted about the change of Prime Minister and it was far from clear to
those outside (or, indeed, to many inside) ministerial circles what had
been at stake between Asquith and Lloyd George. Most Liberal MPs and
the regional Liberal press seem to have remained in a general sense supporters of the government, just as they would have seen it as their duty to
support any government, Liberal or otherwise, in a time of war and
national crisis.[37] Some actions of the Lloyd George ministry worried the
Liberal conscience, but then so had many of Asquith's – including forming a coalition and introducing conscription. It was certainly not clear
that Lloyd George was any less of a Liberal than Asquith, or that Asquith
objected to the new government on the grounds that it had infringed

Liberal principles. Relatively few MPs were deeply committed to Lloyd George before he took office. But, similarly, Asquith could only really count on a loyal cohort of ex-Ministers to follow him at all costs. In between was a vast array of fluctuating opinion. Most MPs simply did not have to declare any sort of allegiance as Asquith refused to consider himself in 'opposition' to the government, and only once (on the Maurice debate) did he take the lead in criticising Lloyd George. No doubt, Asquith felt a more active role would have exposed him to charges of unpatriotic behaviour and being motivated by bitterness. Formally, the party had not split, it was just in the curious position of having one of its most prominent members serving as Prime Minister, while its leader was outside the government. Most Liberals hoped this situation could be resolved, but clearly the longer it went on, the harder that would become.

In the event, once it was clear that Lloyd George had enough support to be Prime Minister, he set about trying to demonstrate how much more dynamic and efficient his regime would be. Supreme power was given to the new War Cabinet of five – Lloyd George, Bonar Law, Arthur Henderson, Milner and Curzon. New ministries were created to tackle labour, blockade, food control, pensions and shipping, focusing on the immediate crises in manpower and food. Figures were recruited from outside politics to fill ministerial jobs, just as Lloyd George had staffed Munitions with 'outsiders'. Herbert Fisher (an academic) took over at Education, Viscount Devonport (a retailer) at Food Control and Sir Joseph Maclay (a shipowner) at Shipping, for instance. This was a new departure, but it should not be overemphasised. The great majority of Ministers were appointed because of their standing in their respective parties, rather than any particular expertise they possessed. A number of weak Liberal Ministers were removed in December 1916, like Harcourt, Tennant and Thomas McKinnon Wood, but their replacements from the Tory ranks were not necessarily any stronger. Not all the 'experts' proved successes, either. Overall, though Lloyd George improved the personnel at his disposal in 1916 it soon became clear that he could not transform the whole machinery of government in the way he had revolutionised Munitions. The constraints on any Prime Minister were formidable, particularly one without a secure party base in the middle of a gigantic war effort.

Lloyd George's new mechanism of government neatly demonstrated these problems. The War Cabinet suffered the same fate as all of the inner committees Asquith had set up.[38] It gradually grew larger as more and more ministers and soldiers were called on to attend or insisted on being present. Instead of dealing only with the most pressing matters it found itself just as clogged with details as Asquith's Cabinet. As its secretary, Maurice Hankey, complained, 'The War Cabinet never discuss their Agenda paper at all…Consequently all the work is dreadfully congested – far worse than it ever was under the so-called "Wait and See" Government.'[39] In effect, decision-making tended to be delegated to yet further committees of the War Cabinet, like the War Policy committee and the 'X' committee, just as it had under Asquith's inner Cabinet. It was at least questionable whether these arrangements were necessarily more efficient than those of the Asquith regime. It does seem that some of the arguments that had racked the previous government had been decided. But this was because the main proponents of a limited war, particularly McKenna and Runciman, had been removed from office, rather than because a new administrative structure had been created. Ostensibly, the new government was committed to mobilising all the nation's resources behind a great effort for military victory. What had not been decided, though, was how this could be done. This task was left to the new Ministries and Ministers created by Lloyd George.

The two great crises facing the government on the home front in early 1917 were food and manpower. Britain still depended to a great extent on imported food and the sinking of merchant ships by German U-boats had produced a critical situation by April 1917.[40] Famously, Lloyd George claimed it was he who personally forced the Admiralty to institute protected convoys of merchant ships, so saving the day. In fact this is a dramatisation of reality. The Prime Minister was one of many voices within and outside the Navy who forced a change of tactics. He could, however, claim the credit for appointing Sir Joseph Maclay to take charge of the new Ministry of Shipping. Maclay eased the imports crisis by requisitioning ships for vital imports, co-ordinating the activities of the docks and the railways and increasing the rate of construction of new merchant ships (despite the Admiralty's obstruction). Food production was also encouraged at home by giving farmers guaranteed prices for corn production, more labour in the form of soldiers, prisoners of war and the Women's Land Army, and threats from county committees that they would be ordered to plough up grassland for wheat. However, Lloyd George had to be careful not to offend the farming lobby. They had powerful friends in the Tory Party and could not be unduly coerced, so, in effect, agriculture was persuaded rather than ordered towards greater cereal production.

The real key to maintaining public faith in the government's handling of the food crisis lay in how it dealt with the distribution of food, though.[41] Many workers were convinced that farmers and retailers were making huge profits out of food shortages and that while they were being made to queue there was no shortage of luxury foods for the rich. Here Lloyd George made a disastrous error in appointing his old subordinate from the Board of Trade, Hudson Kearley (by then Lord Devonport), as Food Controller. As a retailer, Devonport knew all about food distribution, but insisted that it should be left in the hands of shopkeepers like himself to operate a voluntary scheme – a good example of the dangers of appointing an 'expert'. It was not until he was replaced in April 1917 by Lloyd George's even older friend and rival D. A. Thomas (created Lord Rhondda) that the Ministry moved towards price controls and a full-blown rationing system was gradually introduced during 1918. This was the reality behind Lloyd George's successes. Rather than fearless new Ministers ruthlessly organising the country, the new government presented much the same spectacle as Asquith's regime, as it desperately engaged in crisis management, only gradually moving to greater state intervention, and constrained all the time by party bickering and sectional interests.

Still, the manpower question was even more critical for Lloyd George than the food crisis. At the War Office he had called incessantly for more men to be released to the Army and it was the hope that he would give the Army's needs greater priority that had persuaded many Tories to support him as Prime Minister. Lloyd George had not always appeared to support this cause, though. When he was at Munitions he had been equally insistent on the need to supply enough manpower to the armaments industry and it seems that when he called for greater direction of manpower at the end of 1916 he had in mind the efficient use of resources in all sectors of the economy rather than just transferring more men to the Army. Any thoughts of industrial conscription at home were blocked, though, by the need to retain Labour in the coalition and fears of the trade union response. Moreover, the new Ministry of Labour had no role in deciding the allocation of manpower.

In so far as anyone was given this job by Lloyd George, it was Neville Chamberlain (then not even an MP) at the new National Service Department.[42] However, he was not given the authority to arbitrate between the competing needs of the various sectors of the economy and the Army. Indeed, Lloyd George could not give him this authority, for the Army, backed up by its Tory allies, would never have accepted it. Instead, Chamberlain launched a National Service Scheme in February 1917, asking all men undertaking civilian work to register with the government.

Theoretically, they could then be moved to essential jobs and, if necessary, shifted around the country. The scheme proved to be a fiasco and Chamberlain resigned in disgust. Full discussion of the allocation of manpower had to await the arrival of another of Lloyd George's men of 'push and go', Sir Auckland Geddes, at a revamped Ministry of National Service and the deliberations of two new Cabinet committees on war priorities and manpower in 1917–18. As a result, Geddes was given more authority, including the ability to close down non-essential industries and revise certificates of exemption. This introduced more flexibility into the system but hardly solved the central problem of planning the manpower needs of the whole war effort.

The complex history of how the new government faced the difficulties over food supply and manpower are indicative of the harsh realities that faced Lloyd George in December 1916. Behind the rhetoric there was much continuity between the administrations of Asquith and Lloyd George, rather than any great break at the end of 1916. If the government did start to take a more active role in organising the economy it was in 1917–18, under the pressure of a series of crises, rather than immediately on Lloyd George assuming office. Undoubtedly, mistakes were made and it is impossible to know if Lloyd George handled matters more effectively than any rival would have done – certainly his approach was little different in practice to that of Asquith. But the fact remains that crises over manpower, munitions or food supply did not drive Britain out of the war. Enough was done to ensure Britain survived longer than Germany. Moreover, Lloyd George had not been made a dictator in 1916. He was constrained by his Tory allies, a semi-autonomous Army command and the reluctance of powerful interest groups, whether they were trade unions, farmers or shopkeepers to accept direction from a state that had traditionally abstained from detailed intervention in society. The rhetoric of national sacrifice was universal, but most people thought their own interests were exempt.

However, Lloyd George considered his handling of the home front to be only one aspect of his premiership. He gave at least equal weight to his determination to secure overall control of military strategy and to find a way out of the deadlock on the Western Front. He had no wish to be held responsible for further disasters like the Somme. But Lloyd George was never able to fully subordinate the military command, who had important allies in the Tory leadership. What's more, men like Haig were genuinely popular and it would be a huge political risk to try and sack them. Their replacements would be likely to hold the same views anyway.

Gloomily, the War Cabinet concluded 'Haig is the best man we have, but that is not saying much.'[43] In fact, Haig and Lloyd George were very well matched – too well matched to allow either to decisively outmanoeuvre the other. All Lloyd George could do was to attempt to put Haig under the command of various inter-allied co-ordinating bodies, like the Inter-Allied Supreme War Council set up in November 1917.

Lloyd George's other tactic for controlling the generals was to attempt to determine strategy in co-ordination with the other Allied leaders. But, at a meeting in Rome in January 1917, he was unable to persuade the Allies to agree to his personal project for a new attack in Italy to knock Austria out of the war. Instead, Lloyd George turned to the French general, Robert Nivelle, who promised a massive assault on a narrow front in France. Lloyd George hoped this would either bring a quick victory or be shown to be a failure almost immediately, so clearing the way for other strategies. Unfortunately, the Nivelle offensive became bogged down just like all its predecessors. This left Lloyd George in a desperate situation.[44] The French refused to launch another offensive, and the Russian Army had collapsed. The Italians would not attack, either, and though the USA joined the war in April 1917 its troops had yet to arrive. In the summer of 1917 the War Cabinet actually considered the possibility of a peace without victory, the very thing Lloyd George's premiership was meant to forestall. But they concluded this was not realistic, as the Germans refused to consider a genuine withdrawal from Belgium. This meant continuing to fight and the only weapon available to throw at the Germans was the British Army. Thus, Lloyd George felt he had no option but to agree to Haig's plan for a Flanders offensive in July 1917. As a result, Lloyd George ended up presiding over just the sort of bloody stalemate he had wanted to avoid after the disaster on the Somme. The promised victory was further away than ever.

Nevertheless, the disappointments at Passchendaele, closely followed by that at Cambrai, had the ultimate affect of shaking the confidence of the Tory grandees in the military leaders. Lloyd George was able to argue effectively in 1917–18 that Haig could not deliver a quick victory and Britain had no choice but to remain on the defensive until the arrival of massive American armies in 1919. Priority would have to be given to munitions, food and shipping production in order to prepare the country for a long war. Ironically, he had ended up endorsing some of the arguments of McKenna and Runciman that the country could not afford to sustain the kind of war the Army wished to fight – scarcely what Lloyd George had promised anyone in 1916.

   This Fabian strategy was shattered by the Germans' Hindenburg
offensive of March 1918, which brought the blackest moment of the whole
war for Lloyd George. Though the Germans were held back, defeat was
perilously close, and his strategy of concentrating manpower on the
economy rather than the Army appeared seriously mistaken. The question of whether the Army was 'starved' of troops in 1918 (they received
174 000 recruits when they had asked for 334 000) has continued to
exercise historians and has become a subject of fantastic complexity.[45]
Probably both Lloyd George and Haig were at fault in underestimating
the danger in the spring of 1918. But if the British had been defeated,
Lloyd George would have taken the blame. As it was, he faced his most serious domestic challenge of the war, when he was accused by ex-general
Sir Frederick Maurice of lying to the Commons about the relative fighting strength of the Army in France in 1917 and 1918. Asquith scented his
rival's danger and moved a motion of censure. In the ensuing debate,
Lloyd George only survived by exercising the full scope of his parliamentary skills. Essentially, he had misled the Commons, but the matter was so
confused and technical and his own Parliamentary performance so daz-
zling that he was able to rally his supporters. The real issue was who
should be Prime Minister – Asquith or Lloyd George. By 293 votes to 106
the Commons declared there was still no alternative to the original 'man
of push and go'. He had survived to enjoy the fruits of victory.
   But when the Army resumed the offensive under Haig in August 1918,
Lloyd George still refused to believe he could deliver victory and no new
men were released to the Army. Not surprisingly, he failed to appreciate
that Haig had abandoned his 'big push' for the more effective strategy of
a series of short assaults. This, together with American troops and German exhaustion and over-extended lines, finally brought victory. In no
sense could Lloyd George claim that he had contributed a new vision of
strategy that defeated Germany – but then neither had anybody else,
even the generals. More than anything the Allies had just outlasted the
central powers. But Lloyd George's nerve had not cracked; he continued
to believe in victory and to try and organise the nation to achieve that
goal.
   It is perhaps not surprising that Lloyd George did not prove to be a
great military strategist. This has not usually been a requirement for British politicians. Historians have been more surprised that he achieved so
little in the field of domestic reform during his wartime premiership.
After all, this was what he was known for before 1914. But in 1914–18 he
was far too busy trying to win the war to take much interest in continuing

his pre-war career as the great reformer. Even if he had wished to make drastic changes, though, it would have been difficult to persuade his Tory allies to agree. They could always argue that such matters would have to wait until the war was over. The only two major domestic achievements of the wartime Lloyd George government were the Representation of the People Act of 1918, which overhauled the pre-war electoral system and allowed women over thirty the vote, and the 1918 Education Act, which raised the school-leaving age to fourteen. Both had their origins well before Lloyd George became Prime Minister and were in no sense his personal initiatives.

The war ended suddenly, and to most, unexpectedly, in November 1918. The immediate consequence was a huge increase in the Prime Minister's prestige. He became, overnight, 'the man who won the war', an asset of huge significance in 1918, but one that waned quickly as the war receded from the political arena. However, in 1918 he was faced with the immediate problem of how to capitalise on his prestige. He had been planning throughout the year to hold a wartime election on the new franchise and redistribution of seats included in the Fourth Reform Act.[46] The idea was to fight as the wartime coalition of Conservatives, coalition Liberals and the pro-war section of the Labour Party against their critics in Parliament. When the war ended, Lloyd George decided on an immediate election on the same lines. In fact, he had little choice, as the only way he could have reunited with the Liberals was to agree to serve under Asquith, something that neither man was likely to find acceptable. The Conservatives, on the other hand, were willing to agree to Lloyd George continuing as Prime Minister, hoping to capitalise on his prestige and being doubtful about facing the new electorate on their own. They agreed not to oppose 150 Lloyd George Liberals, a generous estimate of the Prime Minister's Liberal following. Labour, though, withdrew from the coalition, determined to fight on their own.

The election was fought in almost total confusion. The electorate had expanded from eight million to 21 million and most constituency boundaries were new. On one side, Lloyd George was in alliance with his old enemies, the Tories and a handful of Labour ministers who refused to leave the coalition. Their programme was studiously vague, made up mostly of appeals to patriotism and some phrases about the need to reward the victorious troops by building a country 'fit for heroes'.[47] In effect, they just asked the electorate to give the coalition that had won the war a chance to sort out the peace. On the other hand were Labour and the Asquithian Liberals. Labour gave more priority to social reform, but had, until a few

weeks before, been part of the coalition. It also contained, to its embarrassment, a very unpopular 'anti-war' wing that included Ramsay Mac-
Donald. The Asquithians were a motley crew. There were few discernible
policy differences between them and the coalition. In fact, most of
Asquith's followers had expected to fight the election as general supporters of the government, as they had been during the war.[48] They were
outraged to find themselves opposed by Conservative or Liberal candidates with the full backing of the Prime Minister. The whole episode
seemed to impugn their patriotism and their contribution to the war
effort. As a result, the election definitely divided the Liberals in a way
1916 had not, because it forced them to take sides. The ensuing bitterness was not healed until both Asquith and Lloyd George had retired
from politics.

   The outcome was a huge triumph for the coalition. Labour only mar-
ginally improved its position to 60 seats, despite fighting on a much
broader front. The 'pacifist' wing was routed. Only about 36 non-coali-
tion Liberals were returned, with all the Asquithian Ministers defeated,
some like Hobhouse and McKinnon Wood losing their deposits. The
official opposition was 73 Sinn Fein MPs from Ireland, who refused to
attend. All the other MPs were Conservatives or Lloyd George Liberals.
This was not a surprising result. The coalition reaped the benefit of post-
victory patriotic fervour and presented itself as an authentic vehicle for
popular aspirations for a better life. It succeeded in being all things to all
voters in the face of a divided and inept opposition. Unfortunately for
Lloyd George a massive victory for the coalition meant a victory for the
Conservatives, who outnumbered his own followers by about 382 to 127.
The pre-war scourge of reaction had ended the war as an effective shield
for the Conservatives from the uncertainties of mass democracy.

4

PEACE-TIME PRIME MINISTER, 1918–22

The post-war coalition government has usually been seen, both by contemporaries and historians, as very much 'Lloyd George's government'. In some ways this is indisputable. The peculiar combination of Tories, Liberals and a few Labour and non-party figures that ruled Britain in 1916–22 would never have come into being but for their decision to support Lloyd George as Prime Minister. Moreover, in 1919 he stood at the height of his authority as one of the three most powerful men in the world, with Georges Clemenceau and Woodrow Wilson. The trappings of power surrounded him, marking him out from his colleagues and setting him at the apex of government. In particular, he continued and extended his usual practice of working with groups of experts, in the Cabinet Office, and the 'Garden Suburb' of special advisers. Senior members of the Cabinet were, in contrast, often treated with contempt, and collectively they sometimes seemed no more than another group of prime ministerial advisers – as when they were all summoned to Inverness in 1921 to meet their Prime Minister, who was convalescing from influenza. Lloyd George also had a tendency to take over the direction of important matters personally, rather than leaving them to departmental Ministers, especially where foreign affairs, the Irish negotiations of 1921–2 or industrial relations were concerned. In all these senses, the government was very much 'his' government.

Even so, the Prime Minister's authority was always constrained, if only by the sheer variety and novelty of the problems the government faced. It was impossible for him to direct, or even be aware of, most areas of government activity. In fields like India or education it is absurd to speak of 'Lloyd George's policy', for he had none. He spent most of his time in office dealing with one crisis after another, switching his attention as the situation demanded. Increasingly it became clear that the Prime Minister's effect on each department of his government was intensive, but short-lived, and his habit of personal intervention meant he was overwhelmed by events rather than orchestrating them. In addition, Lloyd George had to be aware that though he was Prime Minister he led a relatively small minority party, and that his Conservative allies actually had a majority without him. Although this factor finally brought him down in 1922 its influence on his actions varied greatly over time and subject. The Tories felt they *needed* Lloyd George, at least until 1921–2. But, most importantly, the experience of 1916–18 showed there existed a wide area of agreement between Lloyd George and leading Tories and the experience of office tended to bring them even closer.

The government's most pressing problem in 1919 was obviously the post-war peace conference in Paris. Lloyd George set the trend for his premiership by decamping to the Rue Nîtot and leaving his colleagues to run the country for six months. In Paris he was surrounded by an eclectic court of personal advisers, including Hankey, the South African general Jan Smuts, and Philip Kerr from the 'Garden Suburb', rather than members of the Cabinet. His preference for Paris over London was indicative both of his tendency to concentrate on one topic at a time and of an increasing obsession with foreign policy – he spent some 50 per cent of his time on diplomacy even in a less eventful year like 1921.[1] Perhaps, like other Prime Ministers who feel they have conquered their own country, he felt the need for a larger stage on which to conduct his manoeuvres. Certainly, he found peace-making congenial. It offered the perfect opportunity for the sort of face-to-face discussions by the principals that he always favoured to settle disputes.

   Even in the context of Lloyd George's career nothing has generated as much controversy as his aims and achievements in Paris in 1919. A great deal has been elegantly written to demonstrate his unique duplicity, short-sightedness and confusion.[2] It has been claimed that he helped to create a settlement that paved the way for the rise of Nazism and the Second World War by alienating Germany whilst leaving her still potentially the most powerful state in Europe. There is much truth in this, but it was not something any of the peace-makers could do much about, for these problems were already implicit in the outcome of the war and the circumstances of the armistice in November 1918. The Allies were quite clear that they went to Paris as the victors in a war against German aggression, but most Germans did not accept this. They regarded the war as one of defence that had ended in a draw, after which the powers would negotiate a settlement on the basis of President Wilson's Fourteen Points. The Germans were, therefore, bound to be disappointed. It was doubtful, anyway, whether the German Right would have been satisfied with anything less than the mastery of Europe. But Germany had not been devastated and occupied in 1918, only defeated, and would still be a great power, especially as Austria-Hungary and Tsarist Russia had collapsed. To dismember Germany or economically cripple her would have required another war – as it did. Inconclusive wars, like that of 1914–18, rarely lead to satisfactory peaces and Versailles was no exception.

These conundrums were built into the Paris negotiations and could not be resolved, even by Lloyd Georgian ingenuity. However, his personal inclinations did not lead him to differ from the overall trend to produce a peace that aggrieved Germany but still left her powerful. In 1918–19 he felt a great deal of animus against Germany and the Germans. He did not need to be pushed into this by the atmosphere of the coupon election in 1918. Even on Armistice Day he was insistent on the need to put the Kaiser on trial.[3] At Cabinet meetings and in Paris he pressed the matter relentlessly, despite the fact that it was a trivial issue that could only have poisoned the international atmosphere further. Yet, once he was in France, Lloyd George could not resist the role of the great negotiator who would create a lasting settlement and mediate between Wilson and Clemenceau. This inevitably inclined him to favour a moderate peace on some questions, especially over Germany's borders. But these personal preferences were not of overwhelming importance. The Prime Minister did not determine the outcome of the peace in lofty isolation, nor were the broad outlines of British policy a matter of dispute between the Prime Minister and his team of diplomats and advisers. Lloyd George's originality lay in his ability to produce deals to keep the negotiations moving rather than in a unique set of aims.

First, Lloyd George had to secure a minimum set of objectives of immediate concern to Britain.[4] This he achieved with remarkable skill and ingenuity. President Wilson's desire to secure the 'freedom of the seas' for neutral shipping in wartime was sidelined by the proposal that the matter be considered by the future League of Nations. Britain was not dislodged from its possession of the German fleet, though this was less use than it might have been as the fleet scuppered itself at Scapa Flow. Finally, Woodrow Wilson was persuaded to accept British and Dominion control of the German colonies they had occupied, by creating the fiction that they were administered as mandates of the League of Nations. Lloyd George played a central role in this deal by taking up Smuts's concept of a mandate and using him as an intermediary with Woodrow Wilson.

In contrast, Britain's most important aim in Europe was to ensure no one power dominated the Continent. This objective had been achieved simply by the defeat of German ambitions in 1918, the collapse of Russia and the enfeeblement of France. Britain's remaining direct interest in Europe was over reparations. This was the area for which Lloyd George has received the most criticism. It has been claimed that he did not believe in punitive reparations, but cravenly pursued them in order to appease Tory backbenchers, the Northcliffe Press and the impossible demands of the Sumner committee that he had ineptly appointed to estimate Gemany's liability. All sensible men knew reparations were an economic nonsense and, together with the war guilt clause that justified them, ensured Germany could never be reconciled to the peace.[5] In fact, Lloyd George was not much constrained by domestic critics pushing for a harder line on reparations. He faced them down easily enough in the Commons in April 1919. During the General Election he made no specific commitments on the matter, either. Instead, he kept strictly to generalities, like his statement at Bristol on 11 December about Germany 'paying to the limit of her capacity'.[6]

The truth is that Lloyd George, along with most of his delegation, was always determined that Germany would pay a large sum in punitive reparations. Even in his supposedly moderate Fontainebleau Memorandum of 25 March 1919 he insisted Germany must 'undertake to pay full reparations to the Allies'.[7] If her liability was limited to the physical damage caused during the war, then Britain would get virtually nothing. But almost everyone in British politics believed it essential that their country should receive substantial payments from Germany in order to help with Britain's own massive post-war debt to the USA and greatly increased public expenditure. Asquithian Liberals and Labour leaders, as well as Tories, had said this repeatedly during the 1918 election. Most British people believed Germany was an aggressor who should be punished and, despite later criticism, reparations remained very popular in Britain until the Depression in the 1930s made their collection impractical. Lloyd George's personal contribution was, once again, to find suitable formulae for agreement and to promote British interests. By persuading Woodrow Wilson to include dependants' and disability pensions in reparations he raised Britain's share of the payments to a respectable level. This naturally

involved vastly inflating the total, though not as much as Clemenceau
and some people in Britain, like the Sumner committee, wanted. Lloyd
George, too, wanted as much as he could get, but he had to persuade
Woodrow Wilson to agree, and to prevent Germany becoming so desperate that she resumed the war rather than accept the sums being bandied
about.[8] These factors were the cause of his difficulties over reparations in
Paris, rather than an uneasy conscience, domestic criticism or the obviously unviable nature of his plans. His solution was the formula of the war
guilt clause, which established Germany's liability while leaving the
amount open until a later date. This was really a postponement, rather
than a settlement, but it prevented the conference collapsing.

Thus, Lloyd George was not really a 'moderate' over reparations. The
area where he showed flexibility was Germany's borders. This was not a
vital British interest in the way that reparations were. Once its position
was protected, Britain preferred a Europe without disputed borders
(like Alsace-Lorraine in 1871–1914) that might lead to war between the
powers. Britain wished only to reduce its military expenditure and enjoy
its world position in peace. It also disliked the idea of economically crip-
pling Germany by hiving off its most prosperous areas because this
would make it difficult to collect reparations. Most importantly, Lloyd
George had to persuade the Germans to accept the treaty. He could not
scale down reparations, so Germany's borders were the obvious area to
show leniency. Hence Lloyd George's constant hostility to any buffer
state on the Rhine and huge Polish gains at Germany's expense. Lloyd
George had some real success on the latter issue, playing a central role in
making Danzig a free city rather than giving it to Poland and ensuring
plebiscites in Marienwerder and, later, Silesia.[9] This conciliatory attitude
contradicted British policy on reparations, of course, and was unlikely to
actually reconcile Germany to the treaty. Nor did British generosity
extend as far as allowing the Sudeten Germans and Austrians from the old
Austria-Hungary to join Germany. This would actually have made Germany stronger than in 1914. Nevertheless, Lloyd George's refusal to go
along with French plans on the Rhine, or to offer any effective British
guarantee of the French border, left Clemenceau fuming. But no British
Prime Minister could have delivered Britain into France's hands by
unreservedly guaranteeing France's frontiers, nor is it easy to see how any
fudging of the Franco-German borders could have genuinely provided
France with security against a resurgent Germany.

No doubt the Versailles peace settlement was profoundly unsatisfactory,
but it could hardly have been otherwise. Lloyd George's position was

contradictory and sometimes duplicitous, as over his promises to Clemenceau about a guaranteed French border, which failed to materialise. But this reflected Britain's own tortuous position, rather than Lloyd George's uniquely devious agenda. Lloyd George's great achievement was to ensure that there was a peace settlement at all. Time and again it was he who allowed agreement to be reached. He proposed the vital procedural changes on 7 March 1919 in a meeting with Colonel House and Clemenceau that saved the conference from collapse. On subjects as diverse as the size of the German Army to League of Nations mandates he helped promote the ideas that produced the final compromise.[10]

In many ways the Versailles peace treaty was the apex of Lloyd George's career. It is given to few politicians to redraw the map of Europe. The Palace at Versailles was a long way from the schoolroom at Llanystumdwy – a contrast tellingly made on the two sides of the plinth of Lloyd George's statue at Caernarvon. But already it was obvious that Lloyd George's career had taken a different turn to that promised before 1914. He was not necessarily less imaginative, but paradoxically he found himself restricted by supreme power. The problems he faced were so multifarious and intractable that he ceased to be the great innovator and became the great conciliator – the man who produced agreement where none seemed possible, rather than the vehicle of new ideas and approaches. Moreover, though he played less of a lone hand than has been thought in Paris, hubris was setting in. Increasingly impatient of colleagues and convinced of his own powers, cut off from contact with the public and even the House of Commons, he lived within a cocoon of his advisers and sycophants. He had never had many friends in politics. By 1922 he had only rivals.

Paris dominated Lloyd George's thoughts during most of 1919 and his influence on domestic politics was sporadic to say the least. The War Cabinet (reconverted into the Cabinet in October 1919) was, however, able to function fairly harmoniously without him. This was not because it had any clear instructions from the Prime Minister, but because individual Ministers ran their departments without much reference to each other. This naturally helped ease relations at Cabinet level. The second in command was clearly Bonar Law, the Tory leader, but Birkenhead (as F. E. Smith became), Austen Chamberlain and Winston Churchill formed a core of ministers who were active and outspoken on a good many topics.[11] The new post-war problems that it faced meant the Cabinet rarely divided on purely party lines on any subject, other than perhaps free trade, which was just as well as the party balance in the Commons was not reflected in the Cabinet. Though the Tories vastly outnumbered their Liberal allies in Parliament, they only had an 11 to 8 majority in the first post-war Cabinet. This was partly justifiable, though, because the coalition Liberals seemed rather more substantial in 1919 than in 1918, as they had virtually eliminated their Asquithian rivals from the Commons. They certainly made their presence felt on the domestic front. Determined Liberal Ministers like Herbert Fisher at Education and Christopher Addison at Health gave the government a social reforming agenda in these areas that a purely Tory administration would have lacked.

The overarching concern in 1919 was to demobilise the millions of men in uniform without provoking disorder. The War Office had developed an elaborate scheme to release the skilled men first, so reducing the prospect of mass unemployment. Unfortunately this looked much like 'last in, first out' and provoked the very riots and disturbances that the government feared. One of Lloyd George's crucial decisions in 1919 was to appoint Churchill to the War Office in January 1919 with a brief to demobilise the armed forces as soon as possible. Churchill complied and thus determined the government's economic strategy for the next year. Faced with a flood of labour onto the market, Austen Chamberlain, the Chancellor of the Exchequer, acquiesced in the promotion of a post-war boom, deliberately keeping interest rates low.[12] Many of the physical controls on the economy, like rationing and the direction of labour and production in crucial areas, were removed or not enforced, encouraging workers to move to the best-paid jobs and factories to switch to consumer goods as quickly as possible to meet pent-up demand. The alternative of a more regulated transition to peace-time production was never really considered. It was assumed that everyone, employers and employees alike, wanted de-control and the aim was to give people what they wanted. A state-directed economy had only been seriously contemplated if Britain faced an undefeated Germany at the end of the war.

The coalition had also made some noises about building a better world in 1918. The wartime Ministry of Reconstruction had done a good deal of planning for the post-war world in 1917–18, but it was unceremoniously wound up in 1918 and its personnel dispersed. Its files lay gathering dust. But although the government was committed to nothing specific, many Ministers felt they had to do something. Service in the war had greatly expanded the moral claim of the poor to state action to help them. In the background lay the fear that the poor might help themselves to the better world they had been promised if action was not forthcoming. Any government would have had to respond to these considerations, but Lloyd George's produced a peculiar blend of policies.

Lloyd George actually had his own plan for the post-war world. He had outlined this in his first three election speeches in 1918, at Wolverhampton on 23 November, Newcastle on the 29th and Leeds on 7 December, and he prodded his Ministers into action on the subject in 1919.[13] The Prime Minister's big idea was land reform, though on rather different lines to his proposals of 1912–14. Pre-war, Lloyd George had focused on a plan to break Tory and aristocratic domination of the English shires by offering agricultural labourers a minimum wage. This approach was redundant by 1918. Labourers had already received a minimum wage in the 1917 Corn Production Act and the Tories and aristocrats were Lloyd George's allies. However, the war had shown how vital agricultural production was to Britain's safety and wartime food shortages had revived the idea that men could make a good living from the land. Lloyd George proposed that ex-servicemen should be saved from the prospect of unemployment through the offer of state-supplied smallholdings. In response, the government pushed through a Land Settlement Act and a Land Acquisition Act in 1919.

In contrast to 1912–14, nobody was now interested in Lloyd George's proposals. He should have known better, for his earlier Land Campaign had scorned the idea that urban workers would be interested in going 'back to the land', and the slump in agricultural prices in 1920–1 only confirmed the futility of his schemes. This was a portent of Lloyd George's later difficulties. He no longer had time to think through innovative approaches to questions of the day in collaboration with a small group of eclectic advisers – his 1918–19 ideas for land reform were very much an *ad hoc* affair. Perpetual crisis management drained away the creativity that had been so evident before 1914 and Lloyd George consistently appeared to be driven by events rather than imposing his own agenda. As the failed land scheme showed, he was also increasingly out of touch with everyday social realities and only able to look at issues from a governmental perspective. The war had shown agricultural production had to be raised. Therefore, people 'should' be interested in smallholdings. None of these developments augured well for his premiership.

But if Lloyd George was short of ideas, some of his Ministers more than compensated for him. The most dynamic was undoubtedly Christopher Addison, Lloyd George's long-time collaborator, who obtained the post of Minister of the new Department of Health from the Prime Minister as a reward for services rendered. Addison was an enthusiast for housing reform, which consequently became the government's great idea on the home front in 1919. The Urban Land Campaign had identified housing as a pressing need in 1914 and the war had made matters much worse by virtually stopping house-building for four years.[14] Moreover, the rent restrictions of 1915 had severely depressed the incentive to build privately rented housing and in the immediate post-war era builders would wish to concentrate on more lucrative contracts. Addison was thus able to make a convincing case to the Cabinet that drastic state action was needed, backed up by various 'intelligence' reports that the most pressing working-class concern in 1919 was housing. Addison produced the 1919 Housing Act, which required local authorities to draw up plans to remedy housing shortages in their areas. Crucially, they were to receive a state subsidy to cover the gap between the cost of constructing what came to be called council housing and the amount working-class tenants could afford to pay. The Conservatives and more cautious coalition Liberals accepted this financial commitment because they were assured that the Act would merely be a temporary measure to deal with an exceptional post-war crisis. Ironically, the scheme took over 18 months to start delivering any substantial number of houses and proved to be the beginning of the state's large-scale responsibility for housing. But this had not been foreseen in 1919.

Neither had the implications of Addison's other great innovation, the 'out of work' donation to ex-servicemen and civilian workers. This was seen as a back-up to the main policy of engineering a post-war boom to secure full employment and its main aim was to prevent returning heroes being compelled to seek help from the Poor Law, an embarrassment no Minister felt the government could afford. It was non-contributory, set at subsistence level and included dependants' allowances, thus effectively foreshadowing the basic structure of all inter-war unemployment payments. To make the scheme cheaper and less of an obvious expedient, it was converted in 1920 into a greatly extended system of unemployment insurance, covering virtually all workers earning under £250 per annum. Twelve million new workers were covered by unemployment insurance. At a time of full employment this seemed a sensible, cost-cutting plan.[15] When the boom broke, of course, the government was saddled with a huge new responsibility, but, as in housing, this had not been foreseen.

Addison was not the only Minister who extended the government's spending commitments in ways that his colleagues did not fully appreciate.

At Education, Herbert Fisher embarked on a huge programme of school-building and substantially raised teachers' salaries. Worthington-Evans, an enthusiastic member of the pre-war Unionist Social Reform Committee, doubled the level of old age pensions to keep them in line with inflation. None of this was a co-ordinated strategy, let alone one emanating from the Prime Minister, but he raised no objections. The Jeremiah in the Cabinet was, naturally enough, the Chancellor of the Exchequer, Austen Chamberlain. But Lloyd George brushed him aside, 'I think you will have to consider this year as really almost a war condition year' he told the Chancellor.[16] Fiscal responsibility would have to wait on social stability. This attitude was all the easier because military expenditure was rapidly declining from £604 million in 1919 to £111 million in 1922. Rather than occasioning new taxation, social reform just took the place of wartime spending on the Army.

The only area of domestic policy where Lloyd George took direct control at moments in 1919 was industrial relations. The government shared Lloyd George's hope that the wartime collaboration between capital and labour would continue and inspired the grandly titled National Industrial Conference of employers and trade unionists, which met in February 1919 to consider an agreed approach to industrial relations. The reality was rather different, as unions scrambled to maintain wartime gains against rising prices.[17] By late January 1919 strikes were looming or in progress in engineering, shipbuilding, the Tube, railways, mines, and even the police. The government's approach was schizophrenic. Its major political opponent was the Labour Party, a close ally of the unions. The state was still effectively running the coal mines and the railways and faced demands for wage increases in these industries that pitted the authority of the government directly against the trade union movement. Harassed ministers, obsessed with visions of social breakdown and bolshevism in Europe, the colonies and Ireland tended to see Labour and the unions as a conspiracy against civil society and parliamentary government. Lloyd George was not free from these fears by any means and in private and public engaged in some blood-curdling rhetoric about the dangers of socialism. He claimed failure to defeat any miners' strike 'would inevitably lead to a Soviet Republic' and the miners would have to be starved into submission. A national railway strike in September 1919 was denounced as 'an anarchist conspiracy'.[18] This sort of talk substantially worsened industrial relations and contributed to the sense of hysteria with which strike action was regarded by many in right-wing circles in the post-war period. But the government's bark was not accompanied by any bite. Both the miners and railwaymen received compromise wage settlements and the future of the mines was fobbed off onto a Commission headed by a leading judge, Lord Sankey. All these decisions were taken at Lloyd George's instigation. But his Tory colleagues did not demur. They had no stomach for facing hard choices that might provoke the dreaded revolution, especially when the economy was booming and all workers were pushing up their wages.

The apologists for the coalition have tended to view 1919–20 as its golden age, when it offered a positive vision to the country, a genuine attempt to seek a middle way between reaction and revolution, building on the idealism and co-operation between all classes displayed in the First World War. In fact, most historians would now accept that the predominant post-war mood was a desire to return to pre-1914, rather than build a bright new future. Nor was there much yearning for social cohesion as the bitter industrial conflicts of 1919–21 demonstrated. Similarly, the coalition had no real strategy for the post-war world. It just hoped to manage the transition to peace without social meltdown. This approach was shared by both Tories and Liberals and, in effect, all difficult decisions were put off to a later date. The economy was allowed to boom, wage increases were conceded and spending commitments were casually made. Rather than a new social vision, this was a continuation of wartime government. Everything was subordinated to an overriding aim, in this case demobilisation without disorder.

Thus in 1919–20 the government's position on the political spectrum was fluid, or, rather, contradictory. It claimed to be the great bastion of all the forces outside and opposed to the Labour movement, which was vigorously denounced as a hideous Bolshevik conspiracy. Yet, at the same time, the coalition claimed to be a government that represented and worked for all the nation, including the organised working class. In practice, the government could trumpet how much it had done for working people – a booming economy with full employment, no indirect taxes to pay for the war, continued controls on rents, but not wages, even major social reform, like the housing programme. Similarly, the coalition contrived to be simultaneously Liberal and Conservative. Lloyd George could tell his followers that he had helped create the League of Nations at Versailles, rapidly reduced arms spending since 1918, continued wartime temperance legislation and indulged in land reform. He even persuaded the Tories to agree to the disestablishment of the Welsh Church in August 1919, a measure that had been suspended since the outbreak of war and which the Welsh Church accepted in return for a generous disendowment package. Yet he could also tell Conservatives that the Empire had expanded, Austen Chamberlain had introduced a modest amount of imperial preference in his 1919 Budget, building on wartime protectionist measures, and Lloyd George had even abolished his own land taxes of 1909 (they were not bringing in any money as a result of a number of adverse legal decisions). In 1914 Lloyd George had clearly been on the left of British politics. By 1919 he was claiming to be part of the left, right and centre all at once.

This happy situation could not continue for ever and in late 1919 Lloyd George gave some thought to how he could regularise his anomalous position as Liberal Prime Minister of a largely Tory government. His solution was simple enough. The two parties should merge and he would lead the new party. This was not an impossible dream. The Cabinet functioned harmoniously enough and a sizeable group of new, younger MPs of both parties met regularly in the New Members Group, to press for 'fusion' on the grounds that the old party labels were meaningless in the new, post-war world.[19] Lloyd George gave some speeches on the matter in autumn 1919 and put the proposal to his Liberal followers in two meetings on 16 and 18 March 1920. Essentially he urged them to reject their past and embrace a future as a progressive, anti-Labour party, with Addison urging union with the Tories on progressive grounds and Churchill speaking up for an anti-Labour stance. The coalition Liberals were not impressed. To them, the issues of 'the past' were far from dead and the two party meetings Lloyd George addressed started asking awkward questions about free trade, Home Rule, the House of Lords and a host of other matters. Party identity is not easily sloughed off. The Liberals who split from their party over Home Rule in 1886 did not formally join the Conservatives until 1912. Those who became National Liberals in 1931 did not wind up their separate organisation until 1968. Lloyd George was asking his followers to stop being Liberals after less than a year and a half of peace-time co-operation with the Conservatives. Fusion would also cause MPs problems in their constituencies. Most coalition Liberals were supported by Liberal Associations that yearned for Liberal reunion, rather than coalition with the Tories. The fusion plan was dropped before it was even put to the Conservatives. Instead, the coalition Liberals started to create their own regional authorities in 1920, culminating in the launch of a separate National Liberal Party in January 1922. This has often been presented as dismal short-sightedness by Lloyd George's followers, who condemned him to the wilderness when the coalition foundered. But it is by no means certain that the Tories would have accepted fusion in 1920. Lloyd George was reported as claiming 'Bonar is funking it now' when it came to the point of putting the matter to his party.[20] Even if Lloyd George had been leader of a united party in 1922 he could still have been deposed – the Conservatives have little loyalty to leaders who are an electoral encumbrance.

However, the collapse of fusion was an alarming setback for Lloyd George's vision of his future and a harbinger of the difficulties that began to crowd in on him in 1920–1 as it became more and more difficult for the government to continue to be all things to all men. Fiscal policy was one example of these problems. The policy of low interest rates proved impossible to sustain as the government found it increasingly difficult to service its debt.[21] Rates were raised from November 1919 onwards, reaching 7 per cent in March 1920. As this made full employment and public borrowing for social reform more difficult, it became clear that there were limits to the government's continued willingness to appease organised labour and the working class. This was a conclusion Lloyd George himself was coming to by 1920. Rather than being forced into a more conservative stance by his Tory allies, he felt that political circumstances dictated he should set bounds to his government's role as the friend of the worker.

This was clarified during the Cabinet debates over a wealth tax in early 1920. Labour had made much of its plan for a levy on wealth, by which they meant war profiteers, as a solution to the country's huge post-war debt burden. Chamberlain was sceptical, but took the sting out of the controversy by appointing a select committee in February 1920 to look into the matter.[22] It concluded that the government had already done much to tap profits made during the war by continuing its excess profits duty into peace-time at 40 per cent. A levy would raise little and only frighten and alienate business and finance. In Cabinet, Churchill argued strongly that the real case for the levy was political. If the coalition did not adopt the policy it would hand a powerful weapon to Labour and annoy working-class voters. Lloyd George did not agree with Churchill's reasoning. He believed that the government would not win over committed Labour supporters by backing a wealth tax and that it would only provoke hostility from the middle classes and business uncertainty. '[W]e will get nothing out of this tax except disturbance of trade' he told the Cabinet.[23]

This confirmed the decision Lloyd George had made in July 1919 when the Sankey Commission on the coal mines reported. It had,

predictably, split between owners and miners over the question of nationalisation, but Sankey himself favoured public ownership, which therefore
became the Commission's majority recommendation. State involvement
in the mining industry was not without its supporters in the Cabinet.
George Roberts and George Barnes, the two Labour Ministers left over
from the wartime coalition, the *étatiste* Tory Milner and the welfarist Liberals, Addison and Montagu, all argued for some degree of state control.[24] Lloyd George refused to support them and thus prepared the way
for the return of the mines to the private sector in 1921. To Lloyd George
this was not just a matter of taking Tory thinking into account, though it
would have been very difficult to sell any form of nationalisation to Bonar
Law. He believed the mines would be a liability for the government,
involving them in the sort of endless disputes with inflexible miners and
owners with which he had already had to deal.[25]

Nevertheless, his stance on a wealth tax and the coal mines ended any
pretence that his government was left-wing in the circumstances of the
early 1920s. Before 1914, an enthusiasm for redistributive taxation and
welfare spending or nationalisation was only one way of defining someone as left-wing. Many Liberals disliked these things, but believed their
support for free trade, Nonconformity, Home Rule, democracy, temperance and a peaceful foreign policy put them on the left of politics. After
1918, these issues were far from dead, hence the failure of Tory–coalition
Liberal fusion, but disputes about the role of the state in the economy and
the merits of low taxation versus social expenditure became much more
important. Government spending was much higher than pre-war and
the basic rate of taxation was five times higher and affected even skilled
workers. The state ran huge sectors of the economy like the mines and
railways and had to decide what to do with them. For most Tories this was
easy. They were the party of low direct taxes and 'freedom' for the economy (except where tariffs were concerned). Labour (now much more important than before 1914 and the official opposition) stood, somewhat
uncertainly, for the opposite of this. But Liberals found themselves confused and divided. Most of them were fairly close to the Tory position on
taxation and spending. In contrast to the Edwardian era when they had
been happy to tax the landowners and plutocrats, most Liberals balked at
increasing the burden on ordinary middle-class voters. Asquithian leaders
like Runciman and Simon were particularly loud in their calls for
economy and retrenchment. The war also made many Liberals more suspicious of the state and unwilling to countenance nationalisation and
they disliked the way trade union leaders seemed to challenge the elected

government. But Liberals continued to insist that they really were a left-wing party and that taxation and the role of the state were only one aspect of politics.

Lloyd George shared in the confusion of mind of other Liberals. Obviously, he had an impressive record as a social reformer. His government had produced important legislation like the 1919 Housing Act and he had identified himself with a major role for the state in wartime. But the war years also left him with great admiration for the businessmen with whom he had worked and a good deal of antipathy to trade unions, who had often appeared problem-creators rather than problem-solvers.[26] This had only been confirmed by his bruising encounters with them in 1919–20. Lloyd George's time at Munitions also made him much more interested in problems of industrial production and efficiency and this tended to skew his thinking towards the 'business' point of view. Moreover, the Labour Party were his main opponents after 1918, while he worked closely with many leading Tories. All these factors made Lloyd George endorse the doubts of most Liberals about initiatives like a wealth tax and nationalising the mines. They did not believe this transformed them into right-wing figures. But in the context of the political debates of 1920 it did. From mid-1920 onwards the government came increasingly to be perceived as right-wing, and so did Lloyd George.

Ironically for Lloyd George, he was not right-wing enough for many of the government's middle-class supporters and they began to make their discontent felt in 1920–1. Their most potent weapon was an organisation entitled the Anti-Waste League, whose sole purpose was to lower taxes (on hard-working members of the middle class) by cutting expenditure (on feckless workers). The League had influential backing in the popular press and its campaign gathered momentum in late 1920. In the first half of 1921 it won two by-elections and seriously rattled the government. The League's arguments were supported within the government by influential figures like Austen Chamberlain.

After mid-1920, the League had the most powerful ally possible – recession. By the end of 1920 there were over a million unemployed. By the middle of 1921 the total was over two and a half million. Above all else, it was to be the Depression that destroyed the reputation of the coalition and of Lloyd George. The effect on the government was doubly disastrous. Already under heavy criticism for being too left-wing, they suddenly found themselves assailed from the left as the heartless Ministers who presided over the steadily lengthening dole queues. The government began to lose by-elections steadily in working-class areas as

Labour gained five seats from the coalition in 1921 and another four in 1922.

Though criticised from the left and the right, the recession in effect confirmed the coalition's stance on the right of politics. The general view in the Cabinet was that they had no alternative but to embark on a programme of retrenchment, and the government adopted both the logic and the rhetoric of cost-cutting. This was not just a matter of appeasing right-wing critics. Mass unemployment threatened to send expenditure out of control at a time when it was felt industry had to be relieved of tax burdens to aid recovery. Lloyd George did not dissent from this analysis. Neither did anybody outside the Labour movement and even they were silent on other methods of ending the recession. In fact, the Labour conference did not once debate finance or the economy between 1919 and 1922.[27]

The government concluded it had to drop its remaining involvement in running the economy to staunch the flow of public expenditure. Guaranteed wheat and oat prices were withdrawn from agriculture in 1921 – a controversial move, but one most farmers and landowners were probably willing to accept in order to end government controls in farming, especially wages boards for agricultural labourers.[28] More problematically, the coal mines were returned to their owners, so provoking a bitter coal strike from April to July 1921.[29] This time, Lloyd George could not afford to produce a fudge, as in 1919, or in November 1920 when he had persuaded both sides to compromise to end a strike. Lloyd George merely used his ingenuity to play on divisions within the miners' leadership and to separate them from the railwaymen and dockers, so preventing anything approaching a general strike. The legacy of bitterness and social division was enormous. Lloyd George's name became a by-word for deviousness and the betrayal of working people even in South Wales mining areas.

To drive the anti-waste message home the much-publicised Geddes committee was appointed in August 1921 to prune government expenditure. This strategy eventually paid some political dividends as the independent Anti-Waste Party ran out of momentum during 1922. However, middle-class disaffection with the coalition did not disappear, if only because the government had little real success in bringing expenditure and taxation down. Excess profits duty was abolished, because there were no longer any excess profits, but Chamberlain had to impose a 5 per cent corporation tax to balance the budget. Income tax was finally reduced from 6s in the pound to 5s in 1922, but this was still five times higher than the pre-war rate.[30] Inevitably, this situation continued to produce unease,

particularly in the Tory ranks, and to provoke increasing criticism of
Lloyd George's handling of affairs.

The problem was that the government felt it could not make massive
cuts in social expenditure, however much it recognised their theoretical
necessity. A decision was made to halt any further subsidy to new houses
built under Addison's scheme, but, ironically, while it had only produced
600 houses when the government needed them in 1919–20, the scheme
saw the completion of nearly 100 000 in 1920–1, which the Ministry was
committed to subsidise.[31] Unemployment was an even more intractable
difficulty. The government indulged in a good deal of rhetoric against
'shirkers', an attitude embodied in the 'genuinely seeking work' clause of
the 1921 unemployment regulations. But it feared the consequences of
throwing hundreds of thousands of men off unemployment benefit and
onto the Poor Law. It was unlikely that the boards of guardians could have
coped with these numbers and there was a real possibility of widespread
social unrest. The political fall-out would also have been dangerous.
Nobody relished the thought of gallant ex-servicemen in the workhouse in
1922 any more than in 1919. As a result, the government continued to
bail out the national insurance fund. Workers who had exhausted their
entitlement to unemployment insurance were given 'uncovenanted benefit' and dependants' allowances, thus transforming national insurance
into a more acceptable form of out-relief.[32] A Cabinet committee under
Viscount St Davids, an old friend of Lloyd George's, provided over £10
million to local authority public works. Despite all the rhetoric, the Geddes committee proposed only £76 million in cuts, £46.5 million of which
would fall on defence spending. At home it most affected Fisher's
education programme, which few in politics cared about apart from the
Minister and the teachers' unions.

In this situation the coalition had the worst of all worlds. It was blamed
by everyone for the parlous state of the economy, by the middle class for
not cutting taxes and by the working class for trying to. Lloyd George did
all he could to counteract the torrent of criticism by continuing the
favourable relations with the press he had built up in the Edwardian
period. Indeed, Ken Morgan has called his premiership 'one long press
conference'.[33] But the only outlet that was unequivocally pro-coalition
was the *Daily Chronicle*, which had been purchased on the Prime Minister's behalf in 1918. *The Times* and the *Morning Post* were largely critical
and the mass circulation *Daily Mail* and *Daily Express* fickle in their allegiance, despite the Prime Minister's strenuous efforts to court their
owners, Lords Rothermere and Beaverbrook.

By mid-1921 Lloyd George was increasingly gloomy and prone to ill-ness.[34] He was not unaware of the trap into which his government had fallen. But the only way out he could see was to revive the economy, so reducing unemployment and allowing social expenditure to come down. This was not exactly an easy task, but it fitted Lloyd George's increasing concentration on the problem of how to produce wealth, rather than how to ensure its fair distribution. In 1921 Lloyd George spent a good deal of his hard-pressed time thrashing around for solutions to the Depression, mostly with the help of his new acolytes, Edward Grigg and Hilton Young. But they had little success. Businessmen only suggested lower taxes and government expenditure. Economists (Keynes included) were bewildered by the new phenomenon of mass unemployment. The best Lloyd George could do was to agree with the usual analysis that unemployment was due to a collapse of world trade and the only 'solution' was to increase British exports. This meant long-term measures like export credits were the only remedy. Lloyd George announced a suitable package of policies in October 1921, but effectively he could only wait on an upturn in trade.[35] Some improvement followed in 1922, but not enough to revive the coalition's reputation.

Lloyd George was hampered in dealing with the recession by lack of time as well as the intractability of the problems he faced. Much of his energies were channelled into fields where he had little knowledge and fewer interests, but which were a constant source of crises. The most troublesome of these was the Empire, which had expanded enormously in 1914–19, especially in the Middle East, where Britain faced a host of challenges from other colonial powers and nationalist groups. Lloyd George did not object to the expansion of the Empire. Indeed, with the very special exception of the Boer War, where he was motivated by the need to attack a Tory government, he had never shown much anti-Imperial sentiment before 1914. As Ken Morgan has pointed out, this was not an unusual attitude in Wales, where pride in their nation's participation in the benefits of Empire was one of the essential components of Welsh loyalty to the British state.[36] But he had never taken much interest in the colonies and he had remarkably little that was original to contribute to their fate in 1916–22. Usually, he just followed the Colonial Office or Foreign Office line, only to find himself blamed for its many twists and turns. For instance, in the Middle East, Lloyd George inherited conflicting promises to the Arabs, Zionists and French over British intentions, and extensive British ambitions that did not accord with any of these commitments.

The Arabs ended up feeling most betrayed, as they were denied independence in Syria. But it is difficult to discern any time when Lloyd George contributed a distinctive policy line of his own on this matter, or even voiced an opinion.[37]

Much closer to home and even more troublesome was the Irish imbroglio. This had been fudged in the coalition manifesto in 1918, which promised Ireland 'self-government' (which might mean anything from federal devolution through Home Rule to Dominion status) while ruling out any 'coercion' of Ulster, i.e. tending to favour partition if Ireland received anything like Home Rule. Such imprecision was essential because Ireland was likely to cause divisions between Conservatives and coalition Liberals, and Irish politics had been thrown into confusion by the rise of Sinn Fein. In 1918 they won 73 Irish seats, refused to come to Westminster and declared themselves the first Dail Eireann of the Irish Republic. On the same day the IRA began its campaign by killing two policemen.

Lloyd George's pre-1914 position was fairly clear. Like most Liberals, he had favoured Home Rule, with Ulster excluded. Officially, the Conservatives had opposed any sort of Home Rule in Ireland, but in practice they had concentrated their efforts on securing the exclusion of Ulster.[38] Since 1914 Conservative opinion had moved gradually towards accepting Home Rule as long as Ulster was protected. This was partly bowing to the inevitable, but also reflected the willingness of some southern Unionists to try and come to terms with nationalist rule. In 1919 Lloyd George had an even more compelling argument – if Home Rule was not conceded then Sinn Fein would try and take Ireland out of the United Kingdom altogether. The outcome was the Government of Ireland Bill which wound its tortuous way through Parliament in 1919, becoming law in 1920. It provided for two separate Home Rule parliaments, one in Dublin and one in Ulster. Both received substantial local autonomy and a rather nebulous Council of Ireland was set up to deal with matters of mutual concern. Thus, finally, the Conservatives accepted Home Rule in return for the separation of Ulster from the rest of Ireland.

This would have been a generous offer in 1914, but in 1919 it was far too late and Irish opinion had moved on. Even the old Irish Nationalists had campaigned for Ireland to be made a Dominion in 1918. The IRA campaign was stepped up in 1920–1 and the police and army were forced to withdraw to their barracks. Sinn Fein set up its own courts, police force and local government system, showing itself to have at least the acquiescence of most of the population outside Ulster. When, in 1921, elections were held to the Dublin Parliament, provided for under the Government of Ireland Act, Sinn Fein won 124 of the 128 seats, most of them un-opposed.

It is unlikely Lloyd George would have offered a more generous settle-ment to Ireland if he had not been constrained by his Tory allies. He did not have much enthusiasm for Irish nationalism, regarding it as bogus, reactionary and priest-ridden. Lloyd George's model was the way in which the Welsh retained their national pride, while forming an integral part of the United Kingdom. He looked for an Irish leader to come for-ward, as Louis Botha and Jan Smuts had done in South Africa, to recon-cile his people to co-operation with the Empire.[39] Even if this was not possible, Lloyd George had no wish to negotiate from a weak position. The Irish had to take a military drubbing before they could be dealt with at the conference table. Thus he was vocal in his condemnation of the IRA 'murder gang' and in defence of military reprisals, while at the same time a variety of intermediaries were used to probe Sinn Fein's position in 1920–1.

By mid-1921 Lloyd George deemed the time was right. Gradually, he inveigled the Irish leaders into talks with the government. His offer was brilliantly pitched to appease both the Irish and the Tory Unionists. Though his proposals went through a number of subtle changes, the Irish were offered effective independence in the form of a new Dominion on the lines of Canada and Australia, to be called the Irish Free State. Tor-ies were told Ireland would still be part of the Empire, with a Governor-General and bases for the British Navy. In this respect, the uncertain nature of a Dominion's status was most fortunate. The question of Ulster was left unclear, as in 1916. The Belfast Parliament's authority over a separate Ulster, still part of the United Kingdom, was recognised. But a boundary commission was set up to determine its borders. The Irish were assured it would create a tiny, unviable Ulster. Tories were told it would confirm the existing six-county state.

The Irish Treaty of December 1921 was one of Lloyd George's greatest triumphs. Agreement was by no means certain and talks could have broken down at any stage. It is doubtful whether a less talented negotiator could have produced a settlement. The Irish Treaty was certainly not perfect, like the Treaty of Versailles. It produced civil war in the new Free State and created the circumstances for future conflict in Northern Ire-land. But it was about the least worst that could be done in the circum-stances. Once again, Lloyd George confirmed himself as a great negotiator and he could start to hope that the coalition's fortunes might revive on the back of his ingenuity.

Despite his Irish triumph, though, Lloyd George's great passion in
1921–2 remained foreign affairs. Unfortunately for him, events abroad
increasingly ran out of control in this period – a paradigm for his whole
premiership. This was particularly alarming for him because he continued to maintain the impression that foreign affairs were his special prov-
ince and to personalise the conduct of foreign policy. Failure in this field
was, therefore, difficult to blame on anyone else, even the hapless Curzon, the Foreign Secretary. Foreign policy did not bring Lloyd George
down in 1922 but it certainly severely dented his credibility.

Nevertheless, much of what Lloyd George actually did in 1919–21 was
relatively uncontroversial, even in the Foreign Office and the Conservative Party.[40] On the crucial issue of relations with Germany, for instance,
Lloyd George merely continued with the policies outlined at Versailles
and which had widespread support within the coalition. On reparations
he continued to press Germany to pay, even participating in France's
occupation of three towns in the Ruhr in 1921 to force the Germans into
negotiations. But he pressed for more modest amounts than the French
wanted, to ensure German co-operation in making payments. Finally, in
May 1921, the sum of £6600 million was agreed, with Britain receiving 22
per cent of this total. On the other hand, he was flexible about Germany's
borders, helping to secure plebiscites in mainly German areas of Silesia,
rather than ceding them to Poland. As in 1919, the aim was to secure a
'reasonable', prosperous Germany, voluntarily paying its reparations.
This was what most Tories wanted, too.

Even on relations with the Soviet Union, Lloyd George's line was not
very different from that of most of his supporters. Though his ideas
wavered somewhat in 1919, he generally opposed any large-scale intervention in Russia by British troops and favoured a scaling down of the
existing British presence. However much the coalition backbenchers
hated Communism few of them were willing to fight another major war
to defeat it, whatever Churchill thought, and this policy did not meet
much oppositon. The real problem was over trading links with the Soviet
Union because this involved some sort of recognition of the legitimacy of
the Russian regime. Here Tory opinion was divided, the lure of foreign
trade balancing their reluctance to grasp the hands stained with royal
and aristocratic blood. Lloyd George was able to swing the balance decisively in favour of a trade agreement in 1921, even if it produced very
little actual trade.

The real difficulty for Lloyd George in foreign policy came in 1921–2
when he began to gamble on foreign successes to help the coalition's

image at home. This was always dangerous. Foreign events were not within his control, however much he regarded himself as the greatest statesman of his day. He was perhaps encouraged to attempt this, though, by the success not only of the Irish Treaty but of the Washington conference on Pacific fortifications and naval building in November 1921 to February 1922.[41] This was hailed as a great success because it produced plans for a ten-year break in construction, thus saving money, while superficially preserving British relations with both Japan and the USA and burying the fact that Britain had officially abandoned any attempt to preserve world-wide naval supremacy inside a four-power treaty. Lloyd George could not claim much credit for this. He did not attend the conference. What's more, he had argued for the preservation of the exclusive Anglo-Japanese alliance and a large British fleet longer than most in the Cabinet. But this did not stop him basking in the reflected glory of the conference's achievements and dreaming of further restoring his standing at home with an even greater international gathering.

Unfortunately for Lloyd George, his brainchild, the Genoa conference of April 1922, was widely perceived as an unmitigated failure. Lloyd George had personally conceived this idea for a conference of all the European powers, including Germany and the Soviet Union. He built it up in the press and to his supporters as a second Versailles, where Germany and Russia would be welcomed back into the European fold and outstanding differences like reparations finally settled.[42] Personally, he looked forward to recreating the atmosphere of Paris, where all of Europe's great men could meet each other and sort out the Continent's problems behind closed doors. In fact, little was achieved. This outcome had been foreshadowed in Lloyd George's talks with Poincaré in January 1922, when the French Prime Minister had refused to be drawn by the offer of a very nebulous British guarantee of France's frontier with Germany. Even worse from Lloyd George's point of view, Germany and Russia concluded a military and economic agreement at Rapallo. Instead of being reconciled with the rest of Europe, the two 'pariah' nations had joined together. This was a public relations disaster for Lloyd George and was widely trumpeted at home as a decisive defeat. It seemed the man who won the war and made the peace was losing his touch.

This was confirmed by the Chanak crisis of 1922. Lloyd George had backed Greece's ambitions to secure control of large swathes of Anatolia throughout 1920–2. Ken Morgan has shown this was not such a purely personal policy as had been thought.[43] The Foreign Office believed Greece was bound to emerge as the dominant power in the eastern

Mediterranean and wished to have a friendly power in control of the Straits. However, in 1922 the Turks decisively defeated the Greeks and began to advance on the Straits, where a small British garrison was stationed in an international zone set up under the Treaty of Sèvres, signed in 1920 with the old Ottoman Empire. Lloyd George took a publicly bellicose stand, threatening the Turks with war. But on the ground, the local British commander quietly agreed to avoid conflict with the Turkish troops. Once again, Lloyd George had been outmanoeuvred and made to look foolish. Nobody wanted another war, least of all with Turkey. Some Tory Cabinet Ministers, notably Sir Arthur Griffith-Boscawen and Lords Peel, Crawford and Lee disowned his strategy and he was forced to back down – a notable humiliation that marked his weakening hold on the Cabinet. There was a widespread feeling on the Tory benches that Lloyd George had manufactured a crisis over a totally trivial incident in order to whip up a patriotic storm and force the Tories into agreeing to fight another election under the Prime Minister's leadership.

Both Genoa and Chanak were initiated largely for domestic consump-tion but both merely damaged Lloyd George's political standing further. It had been clear since mid-1921 that the coalition was in trouble, as its popularity sank slowly under the weight of the Depression. This was par-ticularly troubling for the coalition Liberals. The 1918 Coupon Election had stereotyped them in working-class seats, many of which were hard hit by the Depression. At by-elections they began to suffer disproportion-ately badly, losing six seats to Labour in 1920–2. At the leadership level they also looked increasingly weak after Addison's removal and the resig-nation of Montagu in March 1922. Their only front-line figure after the Prime Minister was Churchill and his attachment to Liberalism was rather tenuous by 1922.[44]

This development had very serious consequences. It made the coali-tion Liberals look increasingly like a stage army, of little further use to the Tories. Moreover, it made Lloyd George seem less indispensable. Even in Wales, where coalition Liberals had won 18 of the 36 seats in 1918, Lloyd George became an intensely controversial figure, rather than a sort of unofficial President. The coalfields of South Wales, always the area where his appeal was weakest, turned their backs on him and coalition Liberalism after the rejection of the Sankey report and the defeat of the miners in 1921. As a symbol of this, a coalition Liberal whip was beaten in a by-election by a Labour miners' agent at Pontypridd in July 1922. Even in Nonconformist North and Mid Wales, coalition Lib-eralism was no longer the automatic creed of the vast majority. The

Lloyd Georgite candidate only narrowly defeated an Asquithian in a bitter contest in Cardiganshire in February 1921.[45] If Lloyd George could not even be sure of delivering Wales for the coalition he was clearly a waning asset. The Tory Chief Whip, Sir George Younger, made it clear in public in 1921-2, that the party organisation did not wish to fight the next election in alliance with the coalition Liberals and under Lloyd George's leadership.[46] Some Tory Ministers in the Cabinet disagreed with him, but Younger was not reined in. He represented the mood of the party.

⋆ Naturally, some Tories had never been happy with the coalition. But the group of right-wing diehards in Parliament were numerically insignificant, probably no more than 50 MPs, and their leaders were not serious contenders for office. Indeed, some, like Sir Frederick Banbury and Major Gretton, had been noted Parliamentary eccentrics even before 1914.[47] The diehards' best chance of upsetting the coalition had lain in allying themselves with the Anti-Waste bandwagon, but that had ground to a halt by the end of 1921. Some coalition policies, like the Irish settlement, provoked unease in the wider Tory Party, but the leadership faced it down without difficulty at the 1921 National Union conference. The Conservatives were undoubtedly embarrassed by the revelation of the scale of Lloyd George's sale of honours in 1922, but they could hardly break with him on this issue as they were deeply implicated themselves.[48] Essentially, most Tories did not disagree with Lloyd George's policies, however reluctantly they accepted some of them.

What brought the coalition down in 1922 was Lloyd George's decision to push for an election. He hoped patriotic fervour over Chanak and the loyalty of key Tory leaders like Balfour, Austen Chamberlain, Birkenhead and Sir Robert Horne would pull the Tories behind him and win him another mandate. But the party split in the Cabinet, with Griffith-Boscawen, Baldwin and Curzon standing out against a continued coalition. Even then, a more adept leader than Austen Chamberlain might have been able to defeat the rebels, but he referred the decision to fight an election as part of the coalition to a meeting of Tory MPs at the Carlton Club and handled matters badly. The backbenchers refused to follow his lead and they were fortunate in being able to call on Bonar Law as an alternative leader. Law had resigned in 1921 on health grounds but had subsequently made a gradual return to politics. In October 1922 he was available to replace Chamberlain.

The vote at the Carlton Club has been analysed exhaustively, but the reasoning behind many MPs' decisions has proved difficult to pin down.[49] Pro-coalition MPs were usually connected to the government or had seats with a strong Liberal tradition. But the diehards were only a small fraction of the anti-coalitionists. Most MPs who voted against Lloyd George had no deep policy differences with the coalition and were little different in social background to the pro-coalitionists. They were not even hostile to a future arrangement with Lloyd George. They simply felt that the government should be reconstructed to recognise the predominant role of the Tory Party. In particular, there should be a Conservative Prime Minister. Lloyd George no longer had the prestige, the popularity in the country or the followers to remain in that role. By 1922 most Tory MPs felt he was a spent force.

No doubt many MPs also disliked Lloyd George's peculiar style of government, in which he had little contact with backbench MPs. The Prime Minister would only deign to appear in the Commons for question time, twice a week. At all other times he contrived to give the impression that he was far too busy running world affairs to concern himself with Westminster. But there was another important factor behind the rejection of Lloyd George – the almost universal feeling by 1922 that he was totally untrustworthy and unprincipled. This image damaged both his standing with politicians and his appeal in the country. Many Conservative MPs felt that by ditching Lloyd George as Prime Minister they were raising the tone of public life and returning to a mythical pre-1914 golden age of political morality.

People suspected Lloyd George's motives and integrity for all sorts of reasons, some of them justifiable. As the Marconi affair had shown, he was not over-careful in his personal financial dealings, even if he did not use public office to enrich himself directly. The scandal over the sale of honours revived the talk of corruption and some of Lloyd George's entourage, like 'Bronco Bill' Sutherland, press secretary and honours tout, hardly encouraged confidence in their leader's honesty. The whole honours affair seemed sordid and, as the coalition Liberals only existed to support Lloyd George, the line between funding the party and its leader was dangerously blurred. By this time his affair with Frances Stevenson was widely known in political circles, adding the idea that he was a sexual as well as a financial adventurer.

But Lloyd George's conduct of politics also caused disquiet. He was obviously incredibly ambitious and he had never attempted to hide the fact ever since his earliest days in politics. Such unashamed self-seeking often inspired unease. It was often said, for instance, that Lloyd George merely used political associates for his own ends – he was fond of quoting a dictum that he ascribed to Lord Rendel, 'there is no friendship at the top' in politics.[50] Certainly, Lloyd George's political friendships rarely lasted and some close colleagues, like Arthur Lee and Christopher Addison, found themselves unceremoniously dumped when they had outlived their usefulness. His replacement of Asquith in 1916 could be seen as the culmination of this lack of loyalty. As Lord Selborne said of Lloyd George, 'I would never wish to go out tiger hunting with him, not because I doubt his courage but because I know that he would leave anyone in the lurch anywhere if he thought it suited his purpose.'[51] There was a good deal of truth in this. Lloyd George enjoyed political socialising and gossip, but he had no deep need for this sort of male camaraderie. All the emotional support he needed was provided by his domestic circle. Political relationships were, with few exceptions, strictly business.

Lloyd George had also acquired a reputation as someone who did not hesitate to lie. He was well aware of this and could even joke about it. 'This time I have been caught out telling the truth' he told the Tory Whip, Sir George Younger, (probably untruthfully) about the Maurice debate in 1918.[52] This hardly inspired trust from colleagues or the electorate, but Lloyd George was never able to grasp the point of criticism of his honesty. To him it was self-evident that there were many situations in politics where economy with the truth was essential. In delicate negotiations, for instance, he often kept the two principals apart and shuttled between them, telling each side whatever seemed likely to produce an agreement, rather than what was being said. Many who came into contact with Lloyd George, from trade union leaders to Irish Republicans, emerged charmed, but feeling they had been bamboozled.

Perhaps most tellingly, many Conservatives came to the conclusion that Lloyd George had no real political beliefs at all. His only aim was to keep himself in power, and to do that he was ready to betray any principle and perform any political somersault. This was a problem that had dogged Lloyd George since at least 1909–10, when it began to be clear that he was not just another Welsh Radical. That perceptive and, at the time sympathetic, journalist, A. G. Gardiner, had noted then his 'light hold of principles'.[53] His subsequent career had confirmed this view in many people's eyes. Certainly, it seemed bizarre that the great pre-war bugbear of Conservatism had ended up leading a largely Tory government. The coalition had not been a model of consistency either. Lloyd George had fought the trade unions, but also done deals with them. He had denounced the IRA and given Ireland practical independence. Most Tory backbenchers agreed with the necessity of much of this, but found it hard to accept that the Prime Minister seemed to show so little difficulty in changing course when the occasion demanded. It was distasteful to realise that when Lloyd George gave impassioned speeches advocating one course of action, it subsequently transpired that the speech was merely a bargaining counter, not a demonstration of principle. Again, this was a conflict of style. Lloyd George saw his role as the solver of difficulties, not the enunciator of principles. But by 1922 one of the reasons he could not go on making deals was that people did not believe what he said.

The overall verdict on Lloyd George's performance in 1918–22 has to be very mixed. He was increasingly driven by events, rather than seeking to direct them and his most significant achievements were as a deal-maker, particularly at Versailles and over Ireland. These were not great settlements, but without Lloyd George there might not have been any agreements at all. There was actually little that was original in his foreign or colonial policy other than its style. In domestic politics, like most Liberals, he was bewildered by the post-war situation. Asquith's followers liked to claim Lloyd George was no longer a Liberal at all, but it was not very clear what Liberalism stood for after 1918. If Lloyd George compromised some shibboleths, like free trade, he achieved other long-cherished Liberal goals, like Irish Home Rule and Welsh Church disestablishment. He shared the hopes of many Liberals for more social reform in 1919, only to retreat in the face of high taxation and recession. But in 1919–20 he and his coalition Liberal allies created the social framework in housing and unemployment that allowed Britain to weather the 1920s and 1930s without social collapse. This was perhaps the coalition's most lasting domestic achievement. But it left Lloyd George, the great pre-war innovator, marked down in history as a great conservative.

5
TWILIGHT, 1922–45

Historians have varied wildly in their assessment of Lloyd George's career after 1922. The earlier view is that the whole period was a sad post-script to the great years of power. Lloyd George was excluded from office, had no achievements to his name and merely confirmed his repu-tation as a devious power-seeker. However, these ideas were compre-hensively challenged in the 1960s and 1970s. Historians like Robert Skidelsky and John Campbell contrasted the failure of Baldwin and MacDonald to counter unemployment with the imaginative Keynesian solutions Lloyd George propounded, especially in 1928–9.[1] The inter-war period was presented as a conspiracy of dullards to exclude creative politicians like Lloyd George, making him, in Ken Morgan's words, 'a dominant and uniquely creative figure' who 'overshadowed' the 1920s.[2] In turn, this view has more recently been criticised for overlook-ing the problems and confusions in Lloyd George's schemes, thus ensuring that the entire span of his political career is now the subject of debate.[3]

Whether Lloyd George is viewed as a creative force or merely as a poli-tician on the make, his position was extremely difficult in 1922. Most ex-Prime Ministers face one of two futures. If their party is defeated at the polls they become Leader of the Opposition and hope to win the next election. If they are deposed, or resign, from the leadership of their party they face the political wilderness, or at least the House of Lords. But Lloyd George was in neither of these positions. Overnight he had been transformed from Prime Minister to the leader of a small political party, the coalition Liberals. Thus, whilst his career was not over, it was incon-ceivable that his party should ever form a government on its own. His only chance to return to power was to reconstruct the political system in

some way, by allying with another party, splitting one or both of the Conservatives or Labour, or possibly reforming the voting system to give
more weight to minority parties. Thus he was a profoundly destabilising
force in the political landscape of the 1920s – and the legacy of distrust he
inherited from his coalition days did not wane but intensified.

The Conservative leadership was particularly suspicious of their
recent partner in government. When Bonar Law formed his purely Conservative government in October 1922 and called an election, some of
the most senior Tories like Austen Chamberlain, Birkenhead and Balfour refused to serve under Law, raising the prospect of an alternative
leadership and a future deal with Lloyd George. This remained his best
hope after the 1922 election. If the Tories did not gain an overall majority he might be able to offer the Conservatives a new coalition, if necessary
using his Tory allies to force Bonar Law and the irreconcilables to come
to terms. As Lloyd George told his wife, 'I don't care much who gets in as
long as Bonar does not get a working majority.'[4] The resurrection of the
coalition was not complete fantasy. Most coalition Liberals did not face
Conservative opposition in 1922, especially in areas where the Tories
were weak, indicating the continued willingness of some parts of the party
to go on co-operating with Lloyd George. The Carlton Club meeting
had not ruled out any future deals. Many coalition Liberals would have
preferred some form of reunion with the Asquithians, but this was difficult for Lloyd George as Asquith was only prepared to accept his submission, rather than see Lloyd George as co-leader.

Unfortunately, the result of the 1922 election was a disaster for Lloyd
George. His own party's strength was halved to about 60 MPs. Even in
Wales only nine coalition Liberals survived, marking the end of Lloyd
George's political supremacy in the principality. He had visited Wales
less and less from 1916 onwards and the election showed that his influence had shrunk to the rural north west, where his wife ensured the continued loyalty of Caernarvon Boroughs to its old MP. Outside of his old
homeland his name had lost the magic it had held in 1918, and he could
not prevent many of his followers being swept away by Labour's advance
in working-class areas, where coalition Liberalism was damned as surrog-
ate Conservatism.

Labour was able to confirm its role as the major anti-Tory party by winning 142 seats, gradually fanning out from its strongholds in the coalfields. The Asquithians made a modest recovery to about 57 seats and,
regarding themselves as the ascendant force within Liberalism, seemed
less willing than ever to welcome Lloyd George back to the fold on

reasonable terms.The real catastrophe for Lloyd George, though, was that the Tories gained a convincing overall majority, despite winning only 38 per cent of the vote. Bonar Law was confirmed as leader, and Lloyd George's Tory allies remained in the wilderness. The party had no need of a new coalition. Clearly, Lloyd George would have to rethink his strategy, though there seemed no obvious direction for him to go. For want of anything better he continued a desultory intrigue with Chamberlain and Birkenhead, though as time went by the prospects for recreating the coalition looked increasingly dim.

Even more importantly in the long-term, the 1922 election had confirmed the difficult position of all Liberals, coalition and Asquithian, in the face of the rise of Labour to the position of major opposition party. Labour may have had only about 30 seats more than the combined Liberal total but they were united and resolutely anti-Tory – which was more than could be said of the Liberals. Moreover, many of these seats showed every sign of becoming Labour strongholds, particularly in the mining areas. Thus, although Labour's base of support in the organised working class was relatively narrow and unlikely to present them with an overall majority, it was geographically concentrated and solid, making it hard to dislodge them from their role as major opponents of Conservatism. Certainly the Liberals made little impact in most working-class seats in 1922, with both coalition and Asquithian Liberals losing heavily to Labour. In so far as the Asquithians revived in 1922 it was usually in areas where Labour was weak, i.e. suburban and rural seats. Here Liberals could try and construct a winning coalition of anti-Tory voters and, when the Conservatives were unpopular, dissatisfied Tories. But most of these seats were far from safe and were likely to be lost when Conservative voters fled back to their party. The only really safe seats the party had were in rural Wales and north Scotland – hardly enough to secure a major place in British politics. Above all, the rise of Labour increasingly forced all Liberals to define themselves in terms of their relation to the other parties. Were they a sort of non-protectionist Conservative Party or Labour's ally in the cause of progress, as before 1914? Or a sort of 'third way', as yet undefined?

Stanley Baldwin succeeded Bonar Law as Prime Minister in March 1923 without disturbing Tory dominance. In December 1923, probably to reunite his party, he called an election to judge his pledge to introduce tariff reform. This finally bound Chamberlain, Balfour and Birkenhead to their party and scuppered any lingering hopes of a Lloyd George–Tory combination.

Lloyd George was in the USA on a lecture tour when the news broke. At once he knew the old coalition was dead and buried. However, Baldwin's announcement opened up a new political future for Lloyd George.[5] The path to the Tories was blocked but the Asquithian Liberals now had little option but to agree to the return of the prodigal Welshman. If the Liberal Party stood for anything it was free trade and, as in 1903–6, the defence of this shibboleth subsumed all quarrels. Even more pressingly, it seemed Baldwin had given the Liberals a chance to fight on their most favourable ground and regain a position at the centre of politics. The hatchet was buried, for the duration of the campaign at least, and Asquith and Lloyd George campaigned jointly, if not side by side, for the defence of free trade. This most conservative of causes had the strange effect of steering Lloyd George away from the right-wing alliance that had dominated his political life since 1916.

The election saw the Tories sustain heavy losses, going down to 258 seats. But the Liberals failed, just, to become the major anti-Conservative party, with 159 seats to Labour's 191. This was a great improvement on 1922, but there was no disguising the fragility of their position, especially as it was up to the Liberals to decide who would form the next government. Most people who had voted Liberal in 1923 would probably have preferred to see the party strike some sort of deal with the Tories, but this course presented severe difficulties. The Asquithians scarcely had happy memories of the last Liberal–Conservative coalition and any pact with the Tories might lead to the gradual absorption of the Liberals into the Conservative embrace. On the other hand, any Labour government would be sure to frighten off the Tory protest voters of 1923. Even if the Liberals voted against both Tories and Labour and formed their own short-lived government they would find it difficult to prevent opinion polarising around attitudes to Labour.

Lloyd George was back in the councils of the Liberal Party, but he had no more idea than Asquith did about how to extract his party from this dilemma. Asquith initially favoured attempting a minority Liberal government, but Lloyd George argued the party should support Labour in office and Asquith came round to this view.[6] Most of the party were, initially anyway, happy enough with this, especially as it avoided an immediate election. Lloyd George's view, however, marked a further stage in his move away from Conservatism. Possibly he felt he had a better chance of extracting some sort of genuine co-operation in government from MacDonald than from a Tory Party led by Baldwin, his arch-enemy in 1922. However, both he, and the Liberals soon realised they had little to gain from supporting Labour. They refused to consult the Liberals on legislation or to support any reform of the voting system. In the constituencies, hastily formed Labour parties rushed to put up candidates against sitting Liberals – even in Caernarvon Boroughs. Labour only wished to eliminate the Liberals, not co-operate with them.

Lloyd George tacked back to an anti-Labour stance. It was obvious the Liberals' support in the country was slipping away and strong opposition to the government might entice some voters back. He started to attack Labour as closet Bolshevists and persuaded Asquith they must defeat them over their proposed treaty with the USSR. The government was duly defeated, though over the Campbell case rather than the Russian treaty, and an election ensued. Lloyd George pursued his anti-Socialist line in the election, as did most Liberals, but it was impossible for them to seem more anti-Labour than the Tories, especially when they had put Labour in office in January 1924. Probably the most Lloyd George hoped for was another hung Parliament. In fact the Tories won a majority and the Liberals suffered a disaster, being reduced to 40 seats, most of which were held with Tory support. The party had been ground between the millstones as the electorate decided whether or not it wanted a Labour government.

Lloyd George had to bear as much responsibility as Asquith for this disaster. After such a crushing defeat it would be extremely difficult to convince the public that the Liberals were a credible force in politics. The only crumb of comfort he could take from the result was that it finally established his ascendancy over Asquith. Most of the remaining Liberal MPs had survived because they had no Tory opponent and it had been easier for old coalition Liberals to negotiate this kind of deal. Lloyd George had, therefore, the clear support of a majority of Liberal MPs. Asquith had lost his seat and retreated to the Lords. Even more importantly, the Liberal machine was desperately short of money after eight years out of office and three elections in three years. The most realistic source of finance was Lloyd George's political fund, accumulated from the sale of honours in 1916–22. But Lloyd George was only prepared to use it to support the party if it followed his lead. There was certainly plenty of cash available, even though Lloyd George had given £160 000 to the Liberals in 1923–4. The bulk of the fund seems to have been invested in the *Daily Chronicle* newspaper group and when this was sold in 1927–8 it may have netted as much as £2.5 million.[7]

Asquith did not go without a fight, though. He remained leader, while Lloyd George had to be content with being chairman of the Liberal MPs, and in 1926 he made a last attempt to force Lloyd George out. The two men publicly disagreed over the attitude the party should take to the general strike, with Lloyd George arguing for a more conciliatory line. Unfortunately for Asquith, he had misjudged the mood of the party and he found the MPs, the Candidates Association and the National Liberal Federation all more sympathetic to Lloyd George's approach. Finally, in September 1926 he retired, worsted by his old rival. Lloyd George was in control of the party, though he was scarcely popular with the Asquithian diehards who formed themselves into a Liberal Council under Grey to preserve the purity of the Asquithian legacy.

But Lloyd George's main difficulty was to try and formulate a strategy to revive the party from its drastic performance in 1924 and to secure its place in British politics. The fund meant there was no shortage of money, at least, and £300 000 was earmarked to ensure 500 Liberal candidates stood at the next election. Obviously, the party could hardly hope to form a government, but it could try to make gains from the Tories in the sort of rural and suburban seats that the Liberals had won in 1922 and 1923. If Labour also made gains in working-class areas, then there was every chance of another hung Parliament, because it was unlikely Labour could gain an overall majority. This would make the Liberals the kingmakers, as in 1924. But they could not afford to repeat their mistakes of that year. The key was to insist on some form of proportional representation in return for Liberal support. The 1924 election had confirmed that Liberal strength was too geographically diffused for them to win seats in proportion to their percentage of the overall vote. In that election, the Liberals won only 6.5 per cent of the seats in return for 17.6 per cent of the vote. Reform of the electoral system would make the Liberals a crucial feature of a three-party system and probably ensure them a permanent role in government. The Conservatives were extremely unlikely to pay such a high price for Liberal support, but Labour might be willing to bargain as there seemed little hope of an overall majority for them in the near future. Hence, Frances Stevenson's note that 'D's idea is to go definitely towards the *Left*...' [8] At the same time Lloyd George had to ensure that Labour did not feel they could take the Liberals for granted – they had to believe that the Liberals might make a deal with the Tories if they refused Lloyd George's terms. Thus he had to steer a tortuous course throughout 1924–9, aiming to revive Liberalism, sound out Labour about possible co-operation and flirt with Conservatism. But the latter option was largely a feint. As Lloyd George told C. P. Scott, 'Terms would have to include full maintenance of Free

Trade and a reform of the system of voting' and few Tories would agree to that.[9]

This did not make for political consistency – hardly Lloyd George's strong point anyway in the mind of the public and most politicians. Throughout 1924–9 there were rumours and press reports about his negotiations with leading figures in the other parties, particulary Philip Snowden and Winston Churchill (improbably installed as Tory Chancellor of the Exchequer).[10] The only definite conclusion to be drawn from these activities is that Lloyd George had to rule out any sort of pre-election pact with Labour. This was too controversial for the Labour leadership and they could not persuade their local parties to stand down candidates in seats the Liberals might win, even if they had wanted to. Liberal candidates and MPs were left to their own local negotiations with their potential rivals. In public, Lloyd George's attitude to Baldwin's government was much like his policy towards Salisbury and Balfour's governments in 1895–1905 – he opposed everything they did. Thus Baldwin was denounced as too left-wing for continuing the subsidy to the coal industry in 1925 and too right-wing in 1926 over his attitude to the general strike. To Lloyd George the government could do nothing right, whether it was reforming the Book of Common Prayer or the rating system. Again, this did not make for consistency, but it served Lloyd George's purpose of attempting to build the Liberals up as a credible third force, distinguishing them from the Tories and gaining the Liberals much-needed publicity.

But Lloyd George had moved on from the 1890s in some of his concepts of how to conduct political opposition. He was no longer satisfied with purely negative criticism. The Liberals' position in 1924–9 was far more desperate than in 1895–1905, for they had to ensure that the discrediting of the Tories did not just produce more votes for Labour. Lloyd George believed the Liberals had to make a distinctive contribution to political debate and to try and set their own agenda, rather than just responding to the political pronouncements of the two main parties. Above all, they had to banish the idea that they were 'moribund'. 'People will only back a possible winner' he told Frances Stevenson and Liberalism had to look like it could form a government and tackle the country's problems.[11] Moreover, Lloyd George believed that as the 'man who won the war' he *could* solve the big issues of the day and that he genuinely was a more constructive statesman than Baldwin or MacDonald.

Hence Lloyd George instigated the development of a whole raft of new policies for the Liberals in the 1920s and it is on the value of these policies that his posthumous reputation as a great innovative statesman during this period rests. In fact, in tandem with his complex political man-oeuvres in 1922–4, he had already started to turn his mind to the development of policies that would be more relevant to the pressing political questions of the day than those espoused by Asquith. Freed from the constant demands of political office, his mind started to wander over the whole field of political controversy and, to generate new ideas, he again turned, as he had done so often before, to groups of 'expert' advisers. The first fruit of these activities was the most disappointing – a pamphlet entitled *Coal and Power* (1924) on the future of the coal industry. It merely rehashed some of the minority recommendations from Lloyd George's 1919 commission on the coal industry, by suggesting that pits should be organised into groups of producers and the profits pooled. This had been dismissed at the time by both the miners and the owners and was hardly a radical new contribution to the debate.

Much more innovative was *The Land and the Nation* (1925) – on agricultural problems.[12] This contained the conclusions of a committee that Lloyd George had originally appointed in 1923. Some of its ideas had been incorporated in the Liberals' 1924 manifesto, but in an election dominated by Labour and the Zinoviev Letter, nobody seems to have noticed. Meanwhile, Lloyd George upgraded and enlarged the committee in August 1924 and its expanded ideas were presented in *The Land and the Nation* (known as the Green Book), together with a dull companion volume on urban land problems, entitled appropriately the Brown Book, which seems to have gone unread and unheralded. This was not surprising as Lloyd George's attention was focused on the rural constituencies in 1925–6. These were the seats the party might most reasonably expect to win in a future election and he was attempting to outline a bold new programme to secure their allegiance. Above all else, he believed, it was essential to 'strengthen our grasp on the rural districts…'[13] Hard-headed tactics, rather than irrelevant arcadianism lay behind the Green Book.

Moreover, Lloyd George did not just rehash his land programme of 1912–14 or 1919. The Green Book acknowledged that times had moved on. The rapid decline in the number of agricultural labourers made them increasingly marginal figures and rural politics was coming to revolve around the farmers. As they bought their own farms they were less concerned with the iniquities of landlords and more interested in the crisis in agriculture caused by rapidly falling prices. The Green Book proposed an alternative to tariffs. It suggested that the state should take over the ownership of all agricultural land and provide farmers, in return for 'good cultivation' of the land, with security of tenure, extensive technical support and credits. The focus was now on improving economic efficiency, rather than the redistribution of wealth. Nevertheless, while this programme was undeniably modern and appealed to Lloyd George's interest in more efficient farming, it was not rooted in political realities. The farmers disliked it as a further expansion of bureaucratic interference and the Liberal Party was unenthusiastic for similar reasons. Though Lloyd George launched a great campaign to promote the Green Book in 1925 under the auspices of his Land and Nation League, its proposals were watered down to the point of blandness at a special Liberal conference in February 1926. Even the conference's modest plans were still ignored by most rural Liberal parties, though, and by 1928 Lloyd George had all but abandoned the Green Book himself. This illustrated a crucial stumbling block of his approach: how to turn complex ideas about economic efficiency into popular policies.

This problem also haunted Lloyd George's final attempt to make the Liberals 'relevant' at the next election – the Liberal Industrial Inquiry, launched in 1926. By this time he was well aware of the failings of the Green Book and had concluded that only by tackling the central political question of the 1920s – unemployment – could the Liberals start to dictate the political debate and focus attention on themselves. The Inquiry to 'solve' unemployment was partly staffed by savants from the Liberal Summer School (a discussion group set up by progressive Manchester Liberals) and partly by a group of Cambridge economists, of whom Keynes was easily the most renowned and controversial. 'This weekend I have *14* professors at Churt', Lloyd George was able to boast.[14] But, although he gave the inquiry a free hand he was also careful to pack it with political allies and to chair the crucial sub-committee on unemployment himself. It was very much his inquiry, not Keynes's. The result of the inquiry's deliberations was produced in 1928 as *Britain's Industrial Future*, known from its cover as the Yellow Book.

This book's proposals are the key to Lloyd George's post-1922 reputation. It claimed that it was possible to reduce unemployment rapidly to 'normal' levels through the direction of investment to home industries and a series of government loans, totalling over £215 million, to put men to work on a variety of public projects, from road-building to electrification. Even though Keynes advocated these ideas, Lloyd George needed little convincing. He had been suggesting in speeches since the early 1920s that Britain should undertake a programme of necessary public works on its infrastructure to allow the country to take advantage of any recovery. Indeed, his Trade Facilities Act of 1921 had made money available to local authorities and public bodies to do just this.[15]

To a number of historians like Robert Skidelsky and John Campbell this programme appeared to be an enlightened approach to the recession that suggested just the kind of Keynesian remedies that hindsight had shown were necessary to tackle unemployment.[16] However, this view has been strongly challenged. Ross McKibbin pointed out that the Yellow Book did not justify its public works programme on 'Keynesian' grounds, i.e. that putting more men to work would produce a multiplier effect to revive the economy.[17] This justification had not been thought of in 1926–8. Instead, Lloyd George and Keynes claimed that the work they suggested needed doing was essential to the economy and it would be cheaper to use unemployed men to do this than to pay them dole money. This view was open to challenge on all sorts of practical grounds without resorting to a hide-bound 'Treasury view' that any loan raised would divert money from productive enterprises. It was far from clear, for instance, that the country needed all the roads the Yellow Book provided for, that these could be surveyed and built quickly or that huge numbers of the unemployed would be required, suited or willing to work on constructing them. The Labour government of 1929–31, for instance, spent £44.3 million on public works by 1930 and only found work for 61 000 men. The Yellow Book proposals might have employed more, but not enough to 'solve' unemployment.[18]

Thus it was not surprising that many contemporaries were sceptical about Lloyd George's claims. After Keynesian-type remedies signally failed to halt depression in the 1980s many historical economists have come to share these doubts about Lloyd George's plans. They have argued that the Yellow Book ignored the central fact that British industry's problems were rooted in the decline of coal, cotton, steel and shipbuilding. Lloyd George's plans would not have revived these industries and their wider impact might well have been problematic – including a balance of payments crisis and a loss of confidence in the City. Moreover, Lloyd George and Keynes suggested these ideas in 1928–9, when the economy was doing relatively well. Once the economic blizzard hit in 1929–31 both men backtracked. Keynes turned to revenue tariffs and by 1930 Lloyd George had shifted his emphasis to land reform and reducing public expenditure. The Liberal pamphlet, *How to Tackle Unemployment*, of November 1930, suggested that a 10 per cent cut in 'production costs' (wages) and the application of a new Geddes Axe to state expenditure

were required to tackle the Depression. By 1931 all Liberals were calling
for rigid economies and the Yellow Book was heard of no more.[19] So it is
far from clear that Lloyd George had a great plan to solve unemployment
but was thwarted by the small minds of Baldwin, MacDonald and the
British electorate. But at least he was trying to do something and had
obviously not lost his appetite for new ideas to solve immediate problems.

But whatever doubts economists had, most Liberals were willing to
unite behind Lloyd George's plans to fight the 1929 election, with even
Sir John Simon publicly stifling his doubts about the Yellow Book. No
doubt many Liberals did not understand the Yellow Book and their real
enthusiasms lay elsewhere, but they also recognised that Lloyd George
was offering them something to say about the pressing issue of unemployment. A string of six by-election successes in 1927–9 gave the Liberals some hope that they might make a major breakthrough. But close
analysis of the results tended to confirm that the Liberals were making
little headway in industrial areas and even in rural districts they were hampered by the appearance of Labour candidates to split the anti-Tory
vote.[20] The results in 1929 were a bitter blow for many Liberals as they
emerged with only 59 seats, almost all the gains being made from the
Tories in suburban and rural constituencies. In fact, the Liberals had merely undergone a smaller version of their revival in 1922–3, with the electoral system once again denying them seats in proportion to their share
of the national vote. But the great breakthrough remained elusive and
the Yellow Book had not provided the right formula. It had given the
Liberals something to say about how to conquer unemployment, but
popular debate was really about attitudes to the unemployed. Were they
workshy scroungers or victims of capitalism? Lloyd George's scheme was
ingenious but, like the Green Book, it was not harnessed to these wider
social attitudes and political prejudices. Also, the fact that the programme came from Lloyd George did not help its credibility. He had
presided over the beginning of mass unemployment in the early 1920s
and since then his political path had been tortuous, to say the least. The
Yellow Book looked like another desperate expedient to put him back in
power.

Even though the Liberals had not won many seats in 1929 they were
still in a powerful position. Labour won 288 seats, but still needed Liberal
support for a majority. Unlike the situation in 1924, MacDonald intended
to govern for as long as possible to prove Labour's credentials to rule.
There was, therefore, a real chance that Lloyd George could force him to
concede a reform of the voting system in return for the votes of Liberal

MPs. Lloyd George showed that his customary political dexterity had not deserted him in his manoeuvrings with MacDonald.[21] In 1929–30 he showed Labour the Liberals were not in their pockets by conducting talks with Churchill, while not inflicting any crucial defeats on the government in case MacDonald was tempted to call a snap election while his administration was still popular. Once the Depression set in and their popularity plummeted, Labour could only hope to ride out the storm and they became more amenable to a pact with the Liberals. An abortive deal was struck as early as March 1930, only to be overturned by the Labour NEC's intransigence. But in October 1930 Lloyd George was able to extract a promise of voting reform from Labour and the two parties grew closer together in Parliament. A Bill on alternative voting was introduced by MacDonald in 1931 and there were even rumours in July 1931 that Lloyd George would be invited to join the Cabinet. Many in the Labour ranks were impressed with the sixty-eight-year-old ex-premier's enthusiasm and political skill, Hugh Dalton commenting, 'His vitality is amazing and his recent speeches have made a tremendous appeal to our people in the House.'[22] The return from the wilderness was at last within his grasp.

The Liberals' close relations with Labour in 1930–1 caused a good deal of strain within the party, but Lloyd George retained control of his troops. A majority of MPs were willing to accept it in return for the alternative vote and avoiding an election, in which the resurgent Tories would probably retake most of the seats they had lost to the Liberals in 1929. Sir John Simon suggested there was another way out – a pact with the Tories, even if it meant swallowing tariffs. But when he broke with Lloyd George in June 1931 he commanded only two other MPs and a handful of peers. The rest preferred for the moment to cling to Lloyd George as the best hope for Liberalism, however reluctantly. When he was taken ill on the weekend of 25–6 July it seemed no more than a temporary set-back. An operation to remove his prostate was successful and he retired to his estate at Churt to recuperate. However, his hopes of a Liberal–Labour deal were dashed in August 1931 by a new political crisis and the resignation of MacDonald's government when it could not agree on the budget cuts necessary to save the gold standard.

This development presented new opportunies for Lloyd George, even so. The Labour government might be dead, and the possibility of extracting electoral reform with it. But MacDonald proposed a new, temporary government of Conservatives, Liberals and a few Labour figures to implement large-scale cuts. This outcome was not far removed from the course of action Lloyd George had suggested from his sick-bed at Churt.

He had called for more cuts than Labour had been prepared to consider and a Buckingham Palace conference of the party leaders if the government could not agree.[23] If Lloyd George had been fit he would have joined the government. As it was, he accepted his deputy, Herbert Samuel's, action in taking his place in the new Cabinet and Lloyd George's son, Gwilym, was given a minor government post, publicly indicating his father's assent to the new arrangements. This was not pure opportunism on Lloyd George's part. He had abandoned his plans for large-scale public works to solve unemployment and his only real disagreement with the Conservatives' remedies was over tariffs. However, this happy situation was desperately unstable. MacDonald was repudiated by virtually his entire party and left a prisoner of his new Tory allies. They insisted the government should be prolonged into September, and then that it should fight an election against Labour. This was a disaster for Lloyd George. In the existing Commons, the Liberals were necessary to give the government a majority and thus Lloyd George had some influence, even from Churt. But, if the Tories won an overall majority at an election, as there seemed every possibility they would, it was unlikely Baldwin would offer any meaningful job to Lloyd George, even if he retained his Liberal allies.

Lloyd George called on his party to withdraw from the government and fight it at the polls in defence of free trade and the Liberal Party's independence. The only MPs who agreed were Lloyd George's son and daughter, his son's brother-in-law and his future biographer. To a man, the rest refused. They accepted the Conservative analysis that the country's finances were in mortal danger and the overwhelming need was to defeat Labour. Moreover, they all feared for their seats and hoped to avoid a Tory opponent. The party still split between factions led by Samuel and Simon, with the latter offering to abandon free trade and the party's independence if only they would be spared Conservative opposition. At the election, the Conservatives swept the board, with 473 seats, reducing Labour to 52. Their sole allies on the opposition benches were Lloyd George and his family group of four MPs.

This débâcle marked the end of any real possibility that Lloyd George could have played an important role in government. He gave up the chairmanship of the Liberal MPs in disgust. Yet, it could be argued that, rather than being uniquely unfortunate in 1931, he was remarkably lucky from the point of view of his posthumous reputation. Even if economic crisis had not destroyed the Labour government and Lloyd George had taken office in it, he had lost faith in his plans to cure unemployment. If he had been well enough to join the National government, he would have shared responsibility for the expenditure cuts and lost any hope of a reputation as an innovative thinker on economic questions or a figure on the left of British politics. As matters turned out, he could preserve his renown as the 'lost leader' of the 1920s, a dynamic man of ideas who *could* have saved Britain from depression. The real loser in 1931 was the Liberal Party, even though they won 72 seats in the election, thanks to the anti-Labour landslide. They were consigned to the margins of British politics as adjuncts to a Tory-dominated National government. The Simon group in effect became Tories. The 30 or so MPs who accepted Samuel's leadership refused to accept a dose of tariffs and drifted into opposition in 1932–3.

The bleak prospects of the Liberal Party matched those of its ex-leader. Lloyd George was more dispirited than he had ever been after the defeat of 1931 and, for the first time, there were clear signs that his obsessive commitment to political success was waning. He began to take more long holidays in far-flung places like Ceylon and Jamaica and to attend the Commons less and less. He also began to write his *Memoirs* of the First World War, harking back to his days of glory and enjoyably refighting some of his old arguments.[24] Colleagues who Lloyd George particularly disliked for their role in recent events, like Grey and Runciman, received stinging criticism that was startling in the usually dull field of politicians' reminiscences. The result was six very readable volumes, written at great pace and with tremendous verve and style. The combination of vitriol, humour and inspired quotation that characterised Lloyd George's speeches was used to tremendous effect in his writing. The *Memoirs* also contained a good deal of information about Cabinet proceedings – material that other politicians had not been able to use, but which Hankey obtained for his old chief. Lloyd George did not pretend he was writing an impartial account. He was quite open that his *Memoirs* represented a defence of his role in the war and the case that his leadership had been decisive in victory. This meant he was, to say the least, cavalier in his approach to events. It was, for instance, totally misleading to claim that his coalition proposal of 1910 had been primarily inspired by a concern for national defence, that he had no knowledge of the pre-war Anglo-French military discussions or that he had spoken up for British neutrality until the invasion of Belgium. But the heart of the *Memoirs* was an extended critique of the generals and their conduct of the war on the Western Front, especially Passchendaele. The result was a huge furore, that was, no doubt, very good for sales and confirmed a way of looking at the conduct of the war, as a conflict between westerners and easterners, that has been tremendously influential.

The *Memoirs* were also extremely lucrative, earning their author about £65 000. This was a useful supplement to Lloyd George's successful journalistic endeavours. Indeed, he was one of the best-paid writers in the world after 1922. This meant he could live in some comfort and did not have to rely on the generosity of friends, as he had before 1916. Still, he had to maintain two households; his wife in Wales and Frances Stevenson at Churt. Frances bore him a daughter in 1929 and he divided his life between Wales and Surrey, not always entirely amicably, especially because his and Margaret's daughter and political heir, Megan, disliked Frances intensely. Holidays were also problematic and led to endless family rows.

And yet, Lloyd George still hankered for a return to the political limelight. As he told Harold Nicolson in 1932, 'one is never well out of it. One is just out of it.'[25] He decided to make a final attempt to return to the centre stage for the 1935 elections. He had more or less given up on the Liberal Party as 'a complete washout', except in rural Wales.[26] But a run of bad by-election results for the National government in 1934–5 convinced him Labour could stage a great recovery and produce a hung Parliament, or a small National majority. Some of the younger Tories, like Harold Macmillan, were interested in plans similar to his proposals of 1926–9 for economic revival. There were even rumours that Baldwin wanted him to reinvigorate the government. Lloyd George calculated that if he rehashed his old ideas and launched a new campaign, the Cabinet might be persuaded to bring him on board. A group of Welsh industrialists had already asked him in August 1934 to devise a policy to revive Welsh industry, so he was looking into economic policy anyway. He might be able to convince the government that he could win back wavering voters for them and consolidate moderately progressive opinion behind the Cabinet, so giving them victory in a close election. Lloyd George probably hoped for the post of Minister of Reconstruction in a re-formed government.

The means to this end was a great Lloyd George oration at Bangor on 17 January 1935, setting out a 'British New Deal', which looked remarkably like the author's old proposals of the 1920s.[27] This time there was to be peace abroad, rural development and a great 'prosperity loan' to finance work on the roads, railways and telephone service. Baldwin played Lloyd George carefully. He invited him to discuss his ideas with the Cabinet on 18 April, but he had no inclination to include his old rival in the government. Lloyd George realised this fairly quickly and, in response, used £400 000 from his fund to promote a Council of Action for Peace

and Reconstruction. It boasted a motley crew of Nonconformist ministers and centrist thinkers of various kinds and was meant to campaign in
every constituency for Lloyd George's proposals. He talked of slashing
the government's majority and even a deal with Labour in a hung Parliament.[28] But the government were not frightened by this paper tiger.
Without a party organisation behind him, Lloyd George was impotent –
a sort of *reductio ad absurdum* of the problems that had plagued him ever
since he had helped break the Liberal Party in 1916. The Council was
reduced to sending questionnaires to candidates and advising people how
to vote. The Nonconformist conscience stolidly rallied to Baldwin rather
than its old mentor. The whole affair had a distinctly half-hearted and
backward-looking air to it and Baldwin's triumph at the 1935 elections
ended any influence the Council might have had. The Liberals were
reduced to 17 MPs. Their only success was that the Lloyd George group
of four rejoined them, having nowhere else to go. With Lloyd George's
approval, Sir Archibald Sinclair became their new leader.

Lloyd George responded to his failure by retreating deeper into retire-
ment at Churt, only sporadically attending the Commons and confessing
to his secretary, A. J. Sylvester, that running a government department
again would kill him.[29] His last real interest was foreign policy, if only
because the achievement he was most associated with was Versailles. In the
new conditions of the 1930s, Lloyd George became much more amenable to redesigning the Treaty. Indeed, initially, he greatly admired Hitler
as the man who had dragged Germany out of depression and revived its
position in the world. After a visit in 1936 he declared Hitler to be the
'George Washington of Germany'.[30] But he always disliked Mussolini
and the Francoists in Spain and by 1938–9 he was one of the voices calling
for an alliance with Russia to prevent further fascist triumphs.

The outbreak of the Second World War was an ambivalent moment
for Lloyd George. If the government was broadened to one of national
unity, he might, even at the age of seventy-six, expect some sort of post.
But, in his heart, he knew he was too old to recreate his triumphs of
1916–18. The only role he wanted was that of the great statesman who
designs the broad outline of policy, correcting the folly of his younger
rivals.[31] Thus, in October 1939, Lloyd George hinted strongly in a number
of speeches that Britain might gain more from negotiation than from
pursuing the conflict. This did not mean that he was trying to be a British
Pétain. On the contrary, when the conflict started in earnest in April 1940
he urged the need for a vigorous prosecution of the war. But he also
implied that Britain's best course might be to win what advantage it could

and then negotiate from a position of strength. He did not see how an open-ended commitment to war could result in victory when Britain, unlike in 1916–18, stood alone. Thus he simultaneously appealed to politicians who wanted to take the offensive in the war and those who wanted a negotiated peace and, if Churchill's strategy had failed and Russia and America had not been drawn into the war in 1941, Lloyd George might still have played a decisive role in British politics. It was these hopes, as much as his distaste for the routine of office that led him twice to decline to serve under Churchill in 1940. The opportunity did not recur.

Once again, perhaps, it was better for Lloyd George's reputation that he did not take office. On the backbenches he could continue to be the elder statesman, still on good terms with Churchill – after all, he was the only person in Britain who could appreciate the burden a wartime Prime Minister carried. But by 1943 his health was failing rapidly – his last parliamentary vote was cast, appropriately enough for those who see the real Lloyd George as a social reformer, for the Beveridge Report. In 1942 his wife finally died, a tremendous blow that seemed to foreshadow the end. He had bought some land in Llanystumdwy in 1939 and started to build a new home, Ty Newydd, where he clearly intended to die. Detailed instructions were drawn up for his burial by the banks of the Dwyfor and in 1943 he finally married Frances Stevenson, which did nothing to heal family rifts. His last hope was to make a great speech on the peace treaty at the end of the war and, as it was unsure whether he would hold Caernarvon Boroughs again, he agreed to go to the Lords as Earl Lloyd George to provide a forum. The chance of a grand finale never came, for in March 1945 he died, aged eighty-two.

There is little doubt that, whatever historians have decided, Lloyd George felt deeply disappointed by the post-1922 phase of his career. As a politician he was above all a man of action and it was profoundly frustrating to be excluded from office after nearly seventeen years of continuous power. His central problem was that he lacked a powerful enough party base to catapult him back into power. Having broken the party system to achieve the premiership in 1916, he paid the price after 1922, though after all his political wanderings he found his only real home was in the Liberal Party. But even his most ingenious schemes failed to rescue the Liberals from their position as the third force, squeezed between the other two parties. Nevertheless, Lloyd George adapted well to the changed political climate after 1918 – certainly better than any other Liberal leader. He modernised his outlook to tackle the problems of economic decline and the peculiar difficulties of leading a third party. But he could not achieve the breakthrough he needed. Perhaps this was just as well for his reputation, because, though he was more imaginative than most, he did not have the answers to mass unemployment or how to combat Germany's rearmament. His later career may have had an unsatisfactory ending, but at least it has intrigued historians, rather than drawing their censure.

CONCLUSIONS

The most damaging charge laid against Lloyd George has always been that he was merely an opportunist. But contemporary trends in historiography are strongly against the idea that any politician can be satisfactorily viewed purely as a pragmatist whose only concern is power. In recent years, historical inquiry has increasingly focused on unravelling the preconceived ideas and attitudes that underlie political action, and serious attention has been paid to the ideology of even such seemingly unpromising figures as Stanley Baldwin.[1] Lloyd George, though, represents a huge challenge to this approach. His career was so complex and protean that almost any assertion about his approach to politics can be contradicted by reference to some part of his life. There have, though, been attempts to place Lloyd George in a consistent frame of reference, notably by Ken Morgan and Martin Pugh.[2] Morgan tended to see Wales as the most important thread in Lloyd George's career. More recently, Martin Pugh has described Lloyd George as part of a centrist strand of politics, stretching from Joseph Chamberlain to David Owen, which in combining a commitment to social reform with a robust foreign and imperial policy does not fit easily into the party system.

However, Lloyd George's career cannot be contained within these moulds. While he started life as a Welsh politician and returned to Wales to die, his concern for his native land was, at best, intermittent. He preferred Western novels and 'shilling shockers' to Welsh culture and literature. Once he joined the Cabinet in 1905, the political programme he had espoused in Wales receded steadily into the background and after 1916 he visited the place as little as possible.

Similarly, only by carefully selecting from Lloyd George's career can he be made into a consistent 'centrist'. His opposition to the Boer War is hard to square with an imperial vision and, indeed, the Empire meant little to Lloyd George. As Prime Minister, his foreign policy was distinctive in style, but not substance. In fact, it was usually more or less in tune with conventional ideas about the national interest. At home, he was a social reformer, but only in 1908–14 and 1919–20. It is noticeable that those, like John Grigg and Bentley Gilbert, who have undertaken detailed, multi-volume lives of Lloyd George, have been reluctant to try and sum him up under one heading.

This is not entirely surprising. Lloyd George's political life spanned nearly 60 years, during which time the political landscape was transformed. It was perhaps forgivable that he did not display a slavish devotion to principles learned in early life. Moreover, it is exceptionally hard to determine consistent themes in Lloyd George's career because it tended to fall into a number of distinct phases. In the 1890s he was a fairly standard Welsh Radical. In the 1900s he embraced New Liberalism and social reform. Then, in 1914–18, his priority was to achieve victory by mobilising all of the nation's resources. Post-war, his initial acceptance of further social reform was dampened by recession and high taxation. Later, he turned (intermittently) to promoting economic efficiency to solve unemployment.

None of these stages were an inevitable, or even an obvious, progression from their predecessors, and a strong case can be made that Lloyd George's changes of direction were just the response of an ambitious politician to shifting circumstances. But it is also true that all of the phases of his career fitted into a broad Liberal framework, though it was, to say the least, unusual for one man to progress through so many variants of Liberalism and to be in the vanguard of changing the practice of the Liberal Party for over thirty years. If Liberalism was about social reform in 1908–14, for instance, this was at least partly because Lloyd George drove it in that direction. In 1926–31 the Liberal Party's policies were Lloyd George's policies. He also showed a rather inconsistent interest in the fate of the Liberal Party. Though he was its most creative leader before 1914 and in 1925–9 he did not hesitate to split the party in 1916 and in 1920 to try and merge his section of Liberalism with Conservatism. To Lloyd George, the Liberal Party existed to help solve political problems along the lines he approved. Its preservation was not an end in itself.

But if Lloyd George is viewed as a sort of Liberal all his life, this provides a context in which to approach the various stages of his career and the general assumptions on which he acted. First, although his background in Welsh Radicalism did not determine his whole career, there is no doubt that it was vital in shaping some elements in his outlook. Most importantly, he believed in his own image as an outsider in the political elite, whose task was to strike down privilege. He always despised what he called 'the Peacockism of Royalty', for instance, and he never found much to admire in the Anglican Church.[3]

Landowners and the peerage fared little better, and however well he got on with individual members of that class he never showed any trace of succumbing to the aristocratic embrace that Asquith found so comforting. Landowners bore the brunt of Lloyd George-inspired campaigns in 1909–10 and 1913–14 and in the inter-war Green Book he cheerfully proposed to end private ownership of agricultural land. Lloyd George was under no illusions about his popularity with the 'Upper Ten Thousand' and he often alleged that opponents of his plans, like the generals in the First World War, were inspired by 'society' influence. This Radical side of Lloyd George was much less in evidence after 1914, but this was mainly because the political role of the aristocracy and Anglicanism declined so rapidly.

To Lloyd George the antithesis of 'privilege' was 'the people', whose spokesman he was and with whom he could directly communicate through speeches, newspapers and political campaigns. Indeed, the only medium he did not master, towards the end of his life, was radio. His approach to politics was populist, both in the sense that he tried to appeal directly to a mass electorate in a way that could be easily understood and in that he always believed he was representing the interests of most of the people. He had no time for those, like trade union leaders, who claimed to stand between the people and himself, and to interpret their will to him. Anyway, to Lloyd George, 'the people' were a much larger group than the organised working class, stretching from the very poorest to wealthy businessmen. While he disliked social privilege, he also had no respect for what he regarded as purely sectional demands at the expense of the people as a whole. Hence his antipathy to many trade union and Labour Party policies in 1919–22. Lloyd George preferred a consensual approach, where industrial conflicts were ironed out by mediation and agreement – usually with himself as the mediator. To him, workers and employers were essentially on the same side, as constituent parts of 'the people'. Again, this was a common view among his Liberal contemporaries, most of whom were uneasy with notions of conflict at the workplace and the sectional nature of trade unionism.

In the 1890s, Lloyd George's stock in trade was the people's common cause against privilege. But in the 1900s, experience of office revealed to him that the powers of the state could be used to promote the people's welfare. Indeed, the state was Lloyd George's great discovery of the Edwardian period. He found it could be used to promote social reforms that would benefit the many, whilst only penalising the privileged few with increased taxes. This was far from being a unique change of perspective among Liberals. Some Liberal Imperialists and New Liberals had been arguing for a more positive attitude to the state since the 1890s and Lloyd George found plenty of supporters in the Liberal Party for ideas like the People's Budget, National Insurance and his Land Campaign. His unique contribution was to blend social reform with traditional Radicalism, seamlessly combining the old agenda and the new, particularly through his interest in land reform.

Although Lloyd George was a controversial figure among Edwardian Liberals, it was only during the First World War that some of his critics began to accuse him of abandoning Liberalism altogether. His primary aim was undoubtedly to use the state to mobilise the people behind the war effort to ensure victory – an approach that required sacrifices from all for a common goal, even if it meant abandoning some civil liberties. To Lloyd George this was not only essential to win the war, but it was also in line with some of his pre-1914 thinking. For him, there was a real link between a strong state in domestic and defence policy. This approach was a minority view in the party, but it was not unique. All Liberals had to accept a measure of state direction of the economy to ensure victory. Lloyd George merely pushed this approach further and more quickly than many Liberals found it easy to accept, particularly over conscription. But he won the support, even if it was reluctant, of most of the party for his method of conducting the war.

Lloyd George never entirely lost his faith in the state's beneficent role in society (at least if it was directed by him). But it was increasingly contradicted after 1918 by other deeply held opinions. For instance, he also acquired in the 1900s a great deal of respect for businessmen as the creators of wealth and as flexible, open-minded buccaneers in public life, much like himself. This was reinforced by his experience at Munitions, where he worked closely with many entrepreneurs and became deeply involved in trying to create a more efficient armaments industry. In the 1920s, he looked to businessmen to lead the way out of Depression, in partnership with government. His priority became wealth creation and an efficient economy, rather than wealth distribution. But Lloyd George's partial retreat from his enthusiasm for state action can also be seen as part of a general reaction by Liberals as they recoiled from the new realities of higher taxation and economic recession. Most Liberals may not have understood Lloyd George's proposals of 1925–9 very well, but they were prepared to support them because they represented a way of preserving a free trade economy from socialism and tariff reform. This meant that, by the early 1920s, Lloyd George was not on the left, as he had been in the pre-war period. Instead, he tried to create a new identity and relevance for Liberalism as a 'third way' in the centre of politics. Lloyd George was not very successful in this, but his approach at least offered Liberalism some hope for the future.

There is much to be said for understanding the vagaries of Lloyd George's career within the framework of changing Liberal priorities. Nevertheless it has to be recognised that there were elements in his outlook that owed little to Liberalism. Perhaps the most important contradiction was his penchant for dictatorship. For instance, part of the reason behind his admiration for businessmen was his belief in 'leadership' as the way to solve political and economic problems. His success as warleader in the First World War naturally reinforced this feeling in him, until it became almost mystical. He seemed to claim in his *War Memoirs* that virtually every calamity that had befallen the world could have been averted by men, like himself, with the special gift of leadership.[4] Increasingly, he relied on face-to-face meetings with the principals to determine policies and conduct negotiations – a style that reached its apogee at Versailles, but which was replicated in his endless foreign conferences and attempts to solve industrial disputes. His aim was to gather together the men with 'leadership' qualities to search for a decisive solution that would then be presented to the astonished world. Party distinctions meant less and less to him. This had been hinted at as early as his coalition memorandum of 1910, but it became obvious after 1916. All that was necessary was that the men of 'leadership' should work together, excluding the 'pygmies' who infested all political parties.[5] In this context, his admiration for Hitler in the 1930s was not entirely surprising.

This distinctly elitist side to Lloyd George had a much more interesting and constructive aspect as well. It meant that, paradoxically for such a populist, he was rarely constrained by conventional wisdom about what would be popular. His attitude was to identify the central problems facing him, in whatever office he held, and then to look for immediate solutions. For advice he sometimes looked to close colleagues, as in 1916–22, when he enjoyed the company of similarly free spirits like Churchill and F. E. Smith. But, more usually, he sought to pick the brains of expert opinion. Hence his liking for inquiries and groups of advisers. Lloyd George was a professional politician and he took the advice of those with expertise in other fields seriously, whether they were economists, social investigators or businessmen. This meant that he could produce schemes of startling originality, like the Yellow Book in 1928, even if they were not always entirely convincing. But he never worried about whether such ideas would be popular. He believed he represented the people and his skill as a communicator could 'sell' them, whatever scheme he devised. In this he was sometimes mistaken, but it meant he was less constrained by conventional party ideas than virtually any other politician of his time.

In the end, though, what struck many contemporaries about Lloyd George was not so much what he stood for, but his peculiar style of politics. This was not just a matter of his extraordinary personality and charm, to which there are endless testaments. In some ways he helped decisively to modernise the way British politics was conducted. Politics was an obsession for Lloyd George and in the Edwardian era he exemplified the new breed of full-time politicians who were coming to dominate the Commons. His startling, vitriolic and humorous speeches helped democratise communications between politicians and their electorate. But, at the same time, Lloyd George was the first politician to use his own 'think-tanks' of advisers and to work out detailed programmes of policy to present to the electorate. In this, he represented a new approach to politics and a more active role for government in finding solutions to problems.

This was natural enough because Lloyd George was, above all, a constructive politician, who always preferred action to inaction. He saw his role as making deals and producing new ideas to tackle the great issues of the day. This meant he had great achievements to his name, even if he did consistently exaggerate and mythologise his personal role. He could claim a large part in laying the foundations for the mid-twentieth-century welfare state and a substantial contribution to Britain's victory in the First World War, especially through his time at the Ministry of Munitions. After the war he presided over a smooth transition to peace-time and social stability and then produced some imaginative schemes for inter-war reconstruction. At Versailles and in Ireland he did as much as anyone to produce settlements where none might have been achieved. He was a superb orator, an inspirational organiser and an open-minded and courageous political thinker. Perhaps only Winston Churchill of twentieth-century British politicians could say he had achieved as much. The one thing Lloyd George could never inspire for any length of time was trust. He could not convincingly agonise about the need to change course in politics and he rarely maintained a principle in the face of overwhelming adversity. He could not even apologise for his own ingenuity. In other words, he lacked the humbug factor that British politicians so admired. He was too obviously ambitious and contemptuous of conventional ideas about sexual, financial or political morality. It is unlikely he would have felt at home in any British political party in the 1990s.

NOTES AND REFERENCES

Introduction

1. M. Pugh, *Lloyd George* (London: Longman, 1988). C. Wrigley, *Lloyd George* (Oxford: Blackwell, 1992). J. Grigg, *The Young Lloyd George* (London: Eyre Methuen, 1973); *Lloyd George: the People's Champion, 1902–11* (London: Eyre Methuen, 1978); *Lloyd George: from Peace to War, 1912–16* (London: Methuen, 1985). B. Gilbert, *David Lloyd George: the Architect of Change, 1863–1912* (London: Batsford, 1987); *David Lloyd George: Organizer of Victory, 1912–16* (London: Batsford, 1992).
2. Lloyd George to his daughter, Olwen, 2 April 1902, quoted in Wrigley, *Lloyd George*, p. 155.

1 Early Life, 1863–1905

1. H. Spender, *The Prime Minister* (London: Hodder & Stoughton, 1920), p. 81.
2. Quoted in H. du Parcq, *Life of David Lloyd George* (London: Caxton, 1912–13), vol. 1, p. 14.
3. Lloyd George to Lansbury, 16 February 1931, Lloyd George MSS G/11/4/2 (House of Lords Record Office).
4. D. Lloyd George, *War Memoirs*, 2nd edn (London: Odhams, 1938), vol. 1, p. 611.
5. The essential facts are dealt with in Du Parcq, *Life*, vol. 1, pp. 1–51 and W. R. P. George, *The Making of Lloyd George* (London: Faber & Faber, 1976).
6. George, *Making*, p. 46.
7. W. George, *My Brother and I* (London: Eyre & Spottiswoode, 1958), p. 13.
8. Lloyd George diary, 12 November 1881 in Du Parcq, *Life*, vol. 1, p. 40.
9. Lloyd George to Margaret Lloyd George (n.d., probably 1885) in K. Morgan (ed.), *Lloyd George: Family Letters, 1885–1936* (Cardiff and Oxford: University of Wales Press and OUP, 1973), p. 14.
10. Lloyd George diary, 4 September 1887 in Morgan (ed.), *Family Letters*, p. 20.
11. W. R. P. George, *Lloyd George: Backbencher* (Llandysul: Gomer Press, 1983), pp. 72–3, 248–52.
12. K. Morgan, *Rebirth of a Nation: Wales 1880–1980* (Oxford: OUP, 1981), pp. 26–58.

13. J. Hugh Edwards, *The Life of David Lloyd George* (London: Waverly Book Co., 1913), vol. 2, p. 143.

14. R. E. Price, 'Lloyd George and Merioneth Politics 1885, 1886 – a Failure to Effect a Breakthrough', *Journal of Merioneth History and Record Society*, VIII (1975), 301–3.

15. Speech at Blaenau Ffestiniog, 12 February 1886 in Du Parcq, *Life*, vol. 1, p. 77.

16. J. Graham Jones, 'Alfred Thomas's National Institutions (Wales) Bills of 1891–2', *Welsh History Review*, XV (1990), 218–39.

17. George, *Making*, p. 153.

18. Du Parcq, *Life*, vol. 1, pp. 79–83.

19. George, *Backbencher*, p. 96; Grigg, *Young Lloyd George*, pp. 172–4.

20. Grigg, *Young Lloyd George*, pp. 86–171; Gilbert, *Architect of Change*, pp. 77–148 for Lloyd George's early years in Parliament.

21. Lloyd George to William George, 30 October 1890 in George, *Backbencher*, p. 39.

22. Lloyd George to Margaret Lloyd George, 12 August 1890 in Morgan (ed.), *Family Letters*, p. 34 for Healy; Lloyd George to William George, 16 June 1891 in Du Parcq, *Life*, vol. 1, p. 120 for Lloyd George's homework before his early speeches.

23. 3 *Hansard*, CCCXLVIII, cols 904–6.

24. Lloyd George to William George, 20 June 1895 in George, *Backbencher*, p. 174.

25. Lloyd George to Margaret Lloyd George, 19 November 1895 in Morgan (ed.), *Family Letters*, p. 91; Lloyd George to Herbert Lewis, 16 January 1896 in George, *Backbencher*, p. 189.

26. Morgan, *Rebirth*, pp. 59–89.

27. Gilbert, *Architect of Change*, pp. 170–2.

28. Lloyd George to William George, 10 February 1898 in George, *Backbencher*, p. 256.

29. Du Parcq, *Life*, vol. 1, pp. 169–70.

30. George, *Backbencher*, p. 261; Lloyd George to Margaret Lloyd George, 30 August 1898 in Morgan (ed.), *Family Letters*, p. 115.

31. Lloyd George to Margaret Lloyd George, 22 January 1891 in Morgan (ed.), *Family Letters*, p. 40.

32. Lloyd George to Margaret Lloyd George, 2 October 1899 in Morgan (ed.), *Family Letters*, p. 123.

33. George, *My Brother*, p. 187.

34. 4 *Hansard*, LXXXVIII, cols 397–486.

35. Gilbert, *Architect of Change*, p. 202.

36. Du Parcq, *Life*, vol. 2, pp. 332–90. Also, G. E. Jones, 'The Welsh Revolt Revisited: Merioneth and Montgomery in Default', *Welsh History Review*, XIV (1989) 417–37.

37. See especially his article in *The Pilot*, 1 June 1903, quoted in Du Parcq, *Life*, vol. 2, pp. 367–8.

38. George, *Backbencher*, p. 400; Lloyd George to William George, 23 June 1904 in George, *My Brother*, p. 171.

2 New Liberal, 1905–14

1. Gilbert, *Architect of Change*, p. 282.
2. L. Harcourt's Note, quoted in J. Wilson, *CB: A Life of Sir Henry Campbell-Bannerman* (London: Purnell Book Services, 1973), p. 443.
3. For Lloyd George and patronage, J. A. Pease diary, 3 November 1908 in C. Hazlehurst and C. Woodland (eds), *A Liberal Chronicle: Journals and Letters of J. A. Pease, 1st Lord Gainford, 1908–10* (London: Historians Press, 1994), pp. 84–5; for Daniel's elevation, K. W. Jones-Roberts, 'D. R. Daniel, 1859–1931', *Journal of the Merioneth History and Record Society*, V (1965), 58–77.
4. Lloyd George to William George, 11 April 1908 in George, *My Brother*, p. 220.
5. B. Murray, *The People's Budget, 1909/10: Lloyd George and Liberal Politics* (Oxford: OUP, 1980), p. 68.
6. Background in Murray, *People's Budget*, pp. 76–147.
7. Between Asquith's Budget speech on 8 May 1908 and Lloyd George's first Budget in 1909, the Liberals lost four by-elections to the Conservatives and one to Labour.
8. Lloyd George to Sir Robert Chalmers, 5 September 1908, Inland Revenue MSS 73/2 (Public Record Office).
9. J. Ramsden, *The Age of Balfour and Baldwin* (London: Longman, 1978), pp. 94–5, 97; A. Adonis, *Making Aristocracy Work: The Peerage and the Political System in Britain, 1884–1914* (Oxford: Clarendon, 1993), pp. 181–6.
10. C. Hobhouse diary, 10 July 1908 in E. David (ed.), *Inside Asquith's Cabinet: From the Diaries of Charles Hobhouse* (London: John Murray, 1977), p. 72.
11. Spender, *Prime Minister*, pp. 168–9 for the breakfasts.
12. Hobhouse diary, 12 April 1909 in David (ed.), *Asquith's Cabinet*, p. 77.
13. Murray, *People's Budget*, pp. 148–51.
14. Asquith to Venetia Stanley, 13 January 1915 in M. and E. Brock (eds), *H. H. Asquith: Letters to Venetia Stanley* (Oxford: OUP, 1985), p. 378.
15. N. Blewett, *The Peers, the Parties and the People: the British General Elections of 1910* (London: Macmillan, 1972), pp. 68–76.
16. The Liberals retained Dumfries, Cleveland, Mid-Derbyshire and High Peak. The last was the most important, as the swing in a highly marginal seat was kept down to under 1.2 per cent.
17. Du Parcq, *Life*, vol. 4, pp. 686–96.
18. This intimate relationship with the press is chronicled in Ld Riddell, *More Pages From my Diary, 1908–14* (London: Country Life, 1934).
19. Asquith to Venetia Stanley, 26 February 1915 in M. and E. Brock (eds), *Asquith Letters*, pp. 451–2, for the Prime Minister's ranking of his various colleagues.
20. H. Samuel to H. Gladstone, 22 January 1910, Herbert Gladstone MSS, BL Add MSS 45992, fos. 235–6.
21. Blewett, *Peers*, pp. 405–6 for the Liberals' middle-class support in 1910.
22. J. Fair, *British Inter-Party Conferences: a Study of the Procedure of Conciliation in British Politics, 1867–1921* (Oxford: OUP, 1980), pp. 77–102.
23. Reprinted in R. Scally, *The Origins of the Lloyd George Coalition* (Princeton, New Jersey: Princeton University Press, 1975), pp. 375–86.

24. Gilbert, *Architect of Change*, pp. 416–20.
25. B. Gilbert, *The Evolution of National Insurance in Great Britain* (London: Michael Joseph, 1966).
26. See M. Freeden, *The New Liberalism* (Oxford: OUP, 1978); P. Clarke, *Liberals and Social Democrats* (Cambridge: CUP, 1978).
27. H. N. Bunbury (ed.), *Lloyd George's Ambulance Wagon: the Memoirs of W. J. Braithwaite, 1911–12* (London: Methuen, 1957).
28. Vt Esher to O. Brett, 11 December 1911 in M. V. Brett (ed.), *The Journals and Letters of Reginald, Vt Esher* (London: Nicolson & Watson, 1938), vol. 3, p. 75.
29. Differing views of the Edwards case are taken in Grigg, *Young Lloyd George*, pp. 228–39 and George, *Backbencher*, pp. 207–37. George, *My Brother*, pp. 201–2 states that rumours about Lloyd George in *The Bystander* in July 1908 and *People* in January 1909 were reworkings of the Edwards affair.
30. See Grigg, *Young Lloyd George*, pp. 239–45 and *People's Champion*, pp. 127–9. But Grigg's evidence on other affairs is very thin, e.g. *People's Champion*, pp. 182–9. Even R. Lloyd George, *Lloyd George* (London: Frederick Muller, 1960), pp. 53–61 and 105–14 is notably vague about his father's love life.
31. Especially, R. Lloyd George, *Lloyd George*, pp. 221–6 on the highly improbable 'Churt Seraglio'.
32. B. Gilbert, 'David Lloyd George and the Great Marconi Scandal', *Historical Research*, LXII (1989), 295–317.
33. Some of these activities are detailed in George, *Backbencher*, pp. 280–2. Grigg, *Young Lloyd George*, pp. 172–97 first revealed the Patagonian fiasco.
34. G. Searle, *Corruption in British Politics, 1895–1930* (Oxford: Clarendon, 1987), pp. 105–13 deals with these attacks by Conservatives.
35. Grigg, *Peace to War*, pp. 25–33.
36. Morgan, *Rebirth*, p. 124.
37. B. G. Evans to E. T. John, 12 March 1915, quoted in C. Hazlehurst, *Politicians at War, July 1914 to May 1915: a Prelude to the Triumph of Lloyd George* (London: Cape, 1971), p. 223.
38. P. Jalland, *The Liberals and Ireland: the Ulster Question in British Politics to 1914* (Brighton: Harvester, 1980), pp. 58–63, 166–70, 194–200.
39. H. V. Emy, 'The Land Campaign: Lloyd George as Social Reformer, 1909–14', in A. J. P. Taylor (ed.), *Lloyd George: Twelve Essays* (London: Hamish Hamilton, 1971).
40. Hobhouse diary, 17 October 1913 in David (ed.), *Asquith's Cabinet*, pp. 147–8.
41. P. Clarke, 'The Electoral Position of the Liberal and Labour Parties, 1910–14', *English Historical Review*, XC (1975), 828–36; E. Green, *The Crisis of Conservatism: the Politics, Economics and Ideology of the British Conservative Party* (London: Routledge, 1995), pp. 268–70.
42. I. Packer, 'The Liberal Cave and the 1914 Budget', *English Historical Review*, CXI (1996), 620–35.
43. Committee of Imperial Defence, Minutes of 114th Meeting, 23 August 1911, CAB 2/2/9 (Public Record Office) records Lloyd George's knowledge of these discussions.
44. C. P. Scott diary, [4] August 1914 in T. Wilson (ed.), *The Political Diaries of C. P. Scott, 1911–28* (London: Collins, 1970), p. 98; Lloyd George's role in the

crisis has been much discussed, but remains elusive, see K. Wilson, 'Britain' in K. Wilson (ed.), *Decisions for War* (London: UCL Press, 1995).

45. Riddell's diary, 26 October 1912, in *More Pages*, p. 94.
46. K. Morgan, 'Lloyd George and Germany', *Historical Journal*, XXXIX (1996), 755–66.

3 War, 1914–18

1. Primarily by the work of David French, e.g. *British Strategy and War Aims, 1914–16* (London: Allen & Unwin, 1986).
2. Hobhouse diary, 6 April 1910 in David (ed.), *Asquith's Cabinet*, p. 89.
3. Gilbert, *Organizer of Victory*, pp. 93–116.
4. Frances Stevenson diary, 21 September 1914 in A. J. P. Taylor (ed.), *Lloyd George: a Diary by Frances Stevenson* (London: Hutchinson, 1971), p. 2.
5. J. Turner, 'Cabinets, Committees and Secretariats: the Higher Direction of the War' in K. Burk (ed.), *War and the State: the Transformation of British Government, 1914–19* (London: Allen & Unwin, 1982).
6. F. Stevenson diary, 23 October 1916 in Taylor (ed.), *Lloyd George Diary*, p. 118.
7. Lloyd George to Margaret Lloyd George, 30 October 1899 in Morgan (ed.), *Family Letters*, p. 124.
8. Lloyd George to Margaret Lloyd George, 20 October 1914 in Morgan (ed.), *Family Letters*, p. 173.
9. Lloyd George, 'Suggestions as to the Military Position', reproduced in Lloyd George, *War Memoirs*, vol. 1, pp. 219–26.
10. Lloyd George, *War Memoirs*, vol. 1, p. 289.
11. French, *Strategy and War Aims*.
12. D. French, 'The Rise and Fall of Business as Usual' in Burk (ed.), *War and the State*, p. 21.
13. Lloyd George used the phrase to a meeting of bankers and traders, 4 August 1914, T 170/55, Treasury MSS (PRO).
14. C. P. Scott's diary, 14–15 October 1915 in Wilson (ed.), *Scott Diary*, pp. 144–5.
15. Lloyd George, 'Some further considerations on the conduct of the war', 22 February 1915, CAB 37/124/40.
16. Lloyd George in the Commons on 10 March 1915; 5 *Hansard*, LXX, col. 1460.
17. French, 'The Rise and Fall of Business as Usual' for the terms of the debate in 1914–15.
18. Gilbert, *Organizer of Victory*, pp. 139, 171.
19. M. Pugh, 'Asquith, Bonar Law and the First Coalition', *Historical Journal* XVII (1974), 813–36.
20. Bonar Law to Asquith, February 1916, quoted in J. A. Spender and C. Asquith, *Life of H. H. Asquith, Lord Oxford and Asquith* (London: Hutchinson, 1932), vol. 2, p. 230.
21. F. Stevenson diary, 8 February 1915 in Taylor (ed.), *Lloyd George Diary*, p. 29.

22. R. J. Q. Adams, *Arms and the Wizard: Lloyd George and the Ministry of Munitions, 1915–16* (London: Cassell, 1978); C. Wrigley, 'The Ministry of Munitions: an Innovatory Department' in Burk (ed.), *War and the State*.

23. Lloyd George, *War Memoirs*, vol. 1, p. 388.

24. T. Wilson, *The Myriad Faces of War* (Cambridge: Polity Press, 1988), p. 238.

25. Lloyd George's Preface to his collected wartime speeches, *Through Terror to Triumph*, published 13 September 1915. The conscription debate is covered in R. J. Q. Adams & P. Poirier, *The Conscription Controversy in Great Britain, 1900–18* (London: Macmillan, 1987), pp. 89–110.

26. In June 1916 all adult males aged 18–41 were subjected to conscription. The process leading up to this outcome is dealt with in J. Turner, *British Politics and the Great War: Coalition and Conflict, 1915–18* (New Haven and London: Yale University Press, 1992), pp. 64–90.

27. F. Stevenson diary, 18 April 1916, in Taylor (ed.), *Lloyd George Diary*, p. 107.

28. F. Stevenson diary, 12 October 1915 in Taylor (ed.), *Lloyd George Diary*, p. 68.

29. Ld Lansdowne, 'Terms on which a Peace might be considered', 13 November 1916, CAB 37/159/32.

30. Lloyd George, *War Memoirs*, vol. 1, p. 581.

31. F. Stevenson diary, 31 October 1916 in Taylor (ed.), *Lloyd George Diary*, p. 120.

32. F. Stevenson diary, 23 November 1916 in Taylor (ed.), *Lloyd George Diary*, p. 128. Lloyd George's fraught relations with the Army are explored in depth in D. R. Woodward, *Lloyd George and the Generals* (London: Associated University Press, 1983).

33. Gilbert, *Organizer of Victory*, pp. 317–34.

34. Accounts of this process are legion. Some of the more recent are: J. M. McEwen, 'The Struggle for Mastery in Britain: Lloyd George vs Asquith, December 1916', *Journal of British Studies*, XVIII (1978), 131–56; Turner, *Great War*, pp. 112–51; Gilbert, *Organizer of Victory*, pp. 385–419.

35. Ld Selborne, Memorandum, 1916 in D. G. Boyce (ed.), *The Crisis of British Unionism: the Domestic and Political Papers of the 2nd Earl of Selborne, 1885–1922* (London: Historians Press, 1987), p. 188.

36. J. M. McEwen, 'Lloyd George's Liberal Supporters in December 1916: a Note', *Bulletin of the Institute of Historical Research*, LIII (1980), 265–72, points out the caution with which Addison's lists must be treated.

37. G. Bernstein, 'Yorkshire Liberalism during the First World War', *Historical Journal*, XXXII (1989), 107–29.

38. J. Turner, 'Cabinets, Committees and Secretariats' in Burk (ed.), *War and the State*.

39. S. Roskill, *Hankey* (London: Collins, 1970), vol. 1, p. 371.

40. G. de Groot, *Blighty: British Society in the Era of the Great War* (London: Longman, 1996), pp. 86–8.

41. J. Harris, 'Bureaucrats and Businessmen in British Food Control, 1916–19' in Burk (ed.), *War and the State*.

42. D. Grieves, *The Politics of Manpower, 1914–18* (Manchester: Manchester University Press, 1988), pp. 90–148.

43. Hankey diary, 24 February 1917 quoted in G. de Groot, *Douglas Haig, 1861–1928* (London: Unwin Hyman, 1988), p. 298.

44. D. French, 'Allies, Rivals and Enemies: British Strategy and War Aims during the First World War' in J. Turner (ed.), *Britain and the First World War* (London: Unwin Hyman, 1988).
45. D. R. Woodward, 'Did Lloyd George Starve the British Army of Men Prior to the German Offensive of March 1918?', *Historical Journal*, XXVII (1984), 241–52.
46. R. Douglas, 'The Background to the "Coupon" Election Agreements', *English Historical Review*, LXXXVI (1971), 318–36.
47. Turner, *Great War*, pp. 308–29 for the diversity of appeals by Coalition candidates.
48. T. Wilson, *The Downfall of the Liberal Party, 1914–35* (London: Fontana, edn, 1968), pp. 177–81.

4   Peace-time Prime Minister, 1918–22

1. P. Rowland, *Lloyd George* (London: Barrie & Jenkins, 1975), p. 523.
2. Most damning in a huge field is A. Lentin, *Guilt at Versailles: Lloyd George and the Pre-History of Appeasement* (London: Methuen, 1985).
3. Sir H. Wilson diary, 11 November 1918 in C. E. Callwell, *Field Marshal Sir Henry Wilson; His Life and Diaries* (London: Cassell, 1927), vol. 2, p. 149.
4. A. Sharp, *The Versailles Settlement: Peacemaking in Paris, 1919* (Basingstoke: Macmillan, 1991), pp. 16, 124–5, 159–65.
5. Lentin, *Guilt*, pp. 32–80.
6. Quoted in Rowland, *Lloyd George*, pp. 469–70.
7. Lloyd George, 'Some considerations for the Peace Conference before they finally Draft their terms', 25 March 1919, in Lloyd George, *The Truth about the Peace Treaties* (London: Victor Gollancz, 1938), vol. 1, pp. 404–16.
8. Sharp, *Versailles*, pp. 37, 96–7.
9. M. Dockrill and J. D. Goold, *Peace without Promise: Britain and the Peace Conferences, 1919–23* (London: Batsford, 1981), pp. 34–8, 113–18.
10. Sharp, *Versailles*, p. 29; Dockrill and Goold, *Peace*, pp. 43–5, 64–9.
11. K. Morgan, *Consensus and Disunity: the Lloyd George Coalition Government, 1918–22* (Oxford: Clarendon, 1979), pp. 43–4 for the balance of power in the Cabinet.
12. P. Cline, 'Reopening the Case of the Lloyd George Coalition and the Post-war Economic Transition, 1918–19', *Journal of British Studies*, X (1970), 162–75.
13. Rowland, *Lloyd George*, pp. 507–9.
14. K. and J. Morgan, *Portrait of a Progressive: the Political Career of Christopher, Viscount Addison* (Oxford: Clarendon, 1980), pp. 96–113, 122–30.
15. D. Fraser, *The Evolution of the British Welfare State* (London: Macmillan, 1973), pp. 169–72.
16. Lloyd George in Cabinet Memorandum, 25 February 1919, CAB 24/75.
17. R. Lowe, 'The Government and Industrial Relations, 1919–39' in C. Wrigley (ed.), *A History of British Industrial Relations, 1914–39* (Brighton: Harvester, 1987), vol. 2, pp. 189–93.

18. Lloyd George to Bonar Law, 19 March 1919, Lloyd George MSS, F/30/3/31; *The Times*, 29 September 1919.
19. G. Searle, *Country before Party: Coalition and the Idea of 'National' Government in Modern Britain, 1885–1987* (London: Longman, 1995), pp. 117–20.
20. F. Stevenson diary, 16 March 1920 in Taylor (ed.), *Lloyd George Diary*, p. 205.
21. Cline, 'Reopening the Case'.
22. Most recently dealt with in M. Daunton, 'How to Pay for the War: State, Society and Taxation in Britain, 1917–24', *English Historical Review*, CXI (1996), 882–919.
23. Lloyd George in 'Cabinet Conclusions', 4 June 1920, CAB 32/20.
24. Cabinet Minutes, 7 August 1919, CAB 23/15.
25. 5 *Hansard*, CXIX, cols 2000–8 for Lloyd George's speech to the Commons on 18 August 1919.
26. F. Stevenson diary, 25 March, 29 December 1915, 26 May 1917 in Taylor (ed.), *Lloyd George Diary*, pp. 35–6, 87, 159, for anti-trade union sentiments largely absent before 1914.
27. A. Thorpe, 'The Industrial Meaning of "Gradualism": the Labour Party and Industry, 1918–31', *Journal of British Studies*, XXXV (1996), 84–113.
28. A. F. Cooper, 'Another Look at the "Great Betrayal": Agrarian Reformers and Agricultural Policy in Britain', *Agricultural History*, LX (1986), 81–104.
29. C. Wrigley, 'The Trade Unions between the Wars', in Wrigley (ed.), *Industrial Relations*, vol. 2, pp. 93–4.
30. Daunton, 'How to Pay for the War'.
31. Morgan, *Consensus*, p. 95.
32. Fraser, *Welfare State*, pp. 169–72.
33. Morgan, *Consensus*, p. 169.
34. F. Stevenson diary, 31 May, 5 June 1921 in Taylor (ed.), *Lloyd George Diary*, pp. 219–20.
35. *The Times*, 20 October 1921.
36. K. Morgan, 'Wales and the Boer War – a Reply', *Welsh History Review*, IV (1969), 367–80.
37. Dockrill and Goold, *Peace*, pp. 131–79.
38. J. Smith, ' "Bluff, Bluster and Brinkmanship": Andrew Bonar Law and the Third Home Rule Bill', *Historical Journal*, XXXVI (1993), 161–78.
39. D. G. Boyce, 'How to Settle the Irish Question: Lloyd George and Ireland, 1916–21' in Taylor (ed.), *Twelve Essays*.
40. For an overview, A. Sharp, 'Lloyd George and Foreign Policy, 1918–22: the "And Yet" Factor', in J. Loades (ed.), *The Life and Times of David Lloyd George* (Bangor: Headstart History, 1991).
41. J. K. Mcdonald, 'Lloyd George and the Search for a Post-War Naval Policy, 1919' in Taylor (ed.) *Twelve Essays*.
42. Lloyd George hoped Genoa would 'restore his star to the zenith', Riddell diary, 23 March 1922 in Ld Riddell, *An Intimate Diary of the Peace Conference and After, 1918–23* (London: Gollancz, 1933), p. 368.
43. Morgan, *Consensus*, pp. 318–27.
44. Apart from Lloyd George and Churchill there were still six Liberal Cabinet Ministers when the coalition fell – Edward Shortt, Herbert Fisher, Sir Alfred

Mond, Sir Hamar Greenwood, T. J. Macnamara and Robert Munro. But none carried much weight.

45. K. Morgan, 'Cardigan Politics: the Liberal Ascendancy, 1885–1923', *Ceredigion*, IV (1967), 311–46.
46. Ramsden, *Balfour and Baldwin*, pp. 157–60.
47. Crawford diary, 19 November 1910 in J. Vincent (ed.), *The Crawford Papers: the Journals of David Lindsay, 27th Earl of Crawford and 10th Earl of Balcarres, 1871–1940, during the years 1892 to 1940* (Manchester: Manchester University Press, 1984), p. 169 for Gretton.
48. Searle, *Corruption*, pp. 350–76.
49. M. Kinnear, *The Fall of Lloyd George* (London: Macmillan, 1973), pp. 74–91.
50. F. Stevenson diary, 8 August 1916 in Taylor (ed.), *Lloyd George Diary*, p. 114.
51. Ld Selborne, 'Memorandum, 1916' in Boyce (ed.), *Selborne Papers*, p. 188.
52. Crawford diary, 9 May 1918 in Vincent (ed.), *Crawford Papers*, p. 389.
53. A. G. Gardiner, *Pillars of Society* (London: James Nisbet, 1913), p. 290.

5   Twilight, 1922–45

1. R. Skidelsky, *Politicians and the Slump* (London: Macmillan, 1967); J. Campbell, *Lloyd George: the Goat in the Wilderness, 1922–31* (London: Cape, 1977).
2. K. Morgan, 'Lloyd George and the Historians', *Transactions of the Honourable Society of Cymmrodorion* (1972), 80.
3. See the debate between P. Clarke, *The Keynesian Revolution in the Making, 1924–36* (Oxford: Clarendon, 1988), pp. 83–102 and K. G. P. Matthews, 'Could Lloyd George have Done It?', *Oxford Economic Papers*, XLI (1989), 374–407; W. R. Garside, *British Unemployment, 1919–39; a Study in Public Policy* (Cambridge: CUP, 1990), pp. 367–79.
4. Lloyd George to Margaret Lloyd George, n.d. [late November 1922] in Morgan (ed.), *Family Letters*, p. 200.
5. Rowland, *Lloyd George*, pp. 602–3.
6. Scott diary, 5–6 January 1924 in Wilson (ed.), *Scott Diary*, pp. 449–52.
7. F. Owen, *Tempestuous Journey: Lloyd George, his Life and Times* (London: Hutchinson, 1954), pp. 687–94.
8. F. Stevenson diary, 15 May 1926 in Taylor (ed.), *Lloyd George Diary*, p. 246.
9. Scott diary, 7 December 1928 in Wilson (ed.), *Scott Diary*, p. 493.
10. Lloyd George's role in 1924–9 is covered admiringly in Campbell, *Lloyd George: the Goat in the Wilderness*, pp. 107–239 and cynically in P. Williamson, *National Crisis and National Government: British Politics, the Economy and Empire, 1926–32* (Cambridge: CUP, 1992), pp. 22–34.
11. Lloyd George to F. Stevenson, 14 August 1925 in A. J. P. Taylor (ed.), *My Darling Pussy: The Letters of Lloyd George and Frances Stevenson, 1913–41* (London: Weidenfeld & Nicolson, 1975), p. 88.
12. Rural Report of the Liberal Land Committee, 1923–5, *The Land and the Nation* (London: Hodder & Stoughton, 1925). The best analysis of its reception is M. Dawson, 'The Liberal Land Policy, 1924–9', *Twentieth Century British History*, II (1991), 272–90.

13. Lloyd George to F. Stevenson, 20 August 1925 in Taylor (ed.), *My Darling Pussy*, p. 97.
14. Lloyd George to Margaret Lloyd George, 22 September 1926 in Morgan (ed.), *Family Letters*, p. 207.
15. Morgan, *Consensus*, pp. 286–7; Campbell, *Lloyd George: the Goat in the Wilderness*, pp. 193–4.
16. Campbell, *Lloyd George: the Goat in the Wilderness*; Skidelsky, *Politicians and the Slump*.
17. R. McKibbin, 'The Economic Policy of the Second Labour Government, 1929–31', *Past and Present*, LXVIII (1975), 95–123.
18. R. Middleton, 'The Treasury and Public Investment: a Perspective on Inter-War Economic Management', *Public Administration*, LXI (1983), 351–70; A. Booth and S. Glynn, 'Unemployment in the Inter-War Period', *Journal of Contemporary History*, X (1975), 611–36.
19. Skidelsky, *Politicians and the Slump*, pp. 252–5, 335.
20. In 1925–9 there were six by-elections where the winning Tory margin over a second-placed Liberal was smaller than the vote of a third-placed Labour candidate. The best analysis is M. Hart, 'The Decline of the Liberal Party in the Constituencies, 1914–31' (Oxford D.Phil., 1982), pp. 346–52.
21. Williamson, *National Crisis*, pp. 107–17, 203–13, 249–52.
22. H. Dalton diary, 3–5 July 1931 in B. Pimlott (ed.), *The Political Diary of Hugh Dalton, 1918–40, 1945–60* (London: Cape, 1986), p. 147.
23. Williamson, *National Crisis*, p. 324.
24. Lloyd George, *War Memoirs* (London: Nicolson & Watson, 1933–6); see G. W. Egerton, 'The Lloyd George *War Memoirs*: a Study in the Politics of Memory', *Journal of Modern History*, LX (1988), 55–94.
25. H. Nicolson diary, 21 October 1932 in N. Nicolson (ed.), *Harold Nicolson: Diaries and Letters, 1930–9* (London: Collins, 1966), vol. 1, p. 123.
26. F. Stevenson diary, 10 March 1934 in Taylor (ed.), *Lloyd George Diary*, p. 260.
27. S. Koss, 'Lloyd George and Nonconformity: the Last Rally', *English Historical Review*, LXXXIX (1974), 77–108.
28. F. Stevenson diary, 17 July 1935 in Taylor (ed.), *Lloyd George Diary*, p. 312.
29. Sylvester diary, 14 March 1938 in C. Cross (ed.), *Life with Lloyd George: the Diary of A. J. Sylvester, 1931–45* (London: Macmillan, 1975), p. 201.
30. *Sunday Express*, 17 September 1936.
31. P. Addison, 'Lloyd George and Compromise Peace in the Second World War' in Taylor (ed.), *Twelve Essays*.

Conclusions

1. P. Williamson, 'The Doctrinal Politics of Stanley Baldwin' in M. Bentley (ed.), *Public and Private Doctrine* (Cambridge: CUP, 1993).
2. K. Morgan, *Lloyd George* (London: Weidenfeld & Nicolson, 1974); Pugh, *Lloyd George*.

3. Lloyd George to Margaret Lloyd George, 7 August 1890 in Morgan (ed.), *Family Letters*, p. 32.
4. *War Memoirs*, vol. 1, pp. 55–60 for the assessment of Grey's role in 1914.
5. H. Nicolson diary, 6 July 1936 in Nicolson (ed.), *Diaries and Letters*, vol. 1, p. 268.

BIBLIOGRAPHY

Archive collections

Lloyd George MSS: House of Lords Record Office.
Herbert Gladstone MSS: British Library.
Cabinet, Inland Revenue and Treasury MSS: Public Record Office.

Secondary works

Adams, R. J. Q., *Arms and the Wizard: Lloyd George and the Ministry of Munitions, 1915–16* (London: Cassell, 1978).

Adams, R. J. Q., and P. Poirier, *The Conscription Controversy in Great Britain, 1900–18* (London: Macmillan, 1987).

Adonis, A., *Making Aristocracy Work: The Peerage and the Political System in Britain, 1884–1914* (Oxford: OUP, 1993).

Bentley, M. (ed.), *Public and Private Doctrine* (Cambridge: CUP, 1993).

Bernstein, G., 'Yorkshire Liberalism during the First World War', *Historical Journal*, XXXII (1989), 107–29.

Blewett, N., *The Peers, the Parties and the People: the British General Elections of 1910* (London: Macmillan, 1972).

Booth, A. and S. Glynn, 'Unemployment in the Inter war Period', *Journal of Contemporary History*, X (1975), 611–36.

Boyce, D. G. (ed.), *The Crisis of British Unionism: the Domestic and Political Papers of the 2nd Earl of Selborne, 1885–1922* (London: Historians Press, 1987).

Brett, M. V. (ed.), *The Journals and Letters of Reginald, Vt Esher*, 4 vols (London: Nicolson & Watson, 1938).

Brock, M. and E. Brock, (eds), *H. H. Asquith: Letters to Venetia Stanley* (Oxford: OUP, 1985).

Bunbury, H. N. (ed.), *Lloyd George's Ambulance Wagon: the Memoirs of W. J. Braithwaite, 1911–12* (London: Methuen, 1957).

Burk, K. (ed.), *War and the State: the Transformation of British Government, 1914–19* (London: Allen & Unwin, 1982).

Callwell, C. E., *Field Marshall Sir Henry Wilson: His Life and Diaries*, 2 vols (London: Cassell, 1927).

Campbell, J., *Lloyd George: the Goat in the Wilderness, 1922–31* (London: Jonathan Cape, 1977).

Clarke, P., 'The Electoral Position of the Liberal and Labour Parties, 1910–14', *English Historical Review*, XC (1975), 828–36.

—— *Liberals and Social Democrats* (Cambridge: CUP, 1978).

—— *The Keynesian Revolution in the Making, 1924–36* (Oxford: Clarendon, 1988).

Cline, P., 'Reopening the Case of the Lloyd George Coalition and the Postwar Economic Transition, 1918–19', *Journal of British Studies*, X (1970), 162–75.

Cooper, A. F., 'Another Look at the "Great Betrayal": Agrarian Reformers and Agricultural Policy in Britain', *Agricultural History*, LX (1986), 81–104.

Cross, C. (ed.), *Life with Lloyd George: the Diary of A. J. Sylvester, 1931–45* (London: Macmillan, 1975).

Daunton, M., 'How to Pay for the War: State, Society and Taxation in Britain, 1917–24', *English Historical Review*, CXI (1996), 882–919.

David, E. (ed.), *Inside Asquith's Cabinet: From the Diaries of Charles Hobhouse* (London: John Murray, 1977).

Dawson, M., 'The Liberal Land Policy, 1924–9', *Twentieth Century British History*, II (1991), 272–90.

de Groot, G., *Douglas Haig, 1861–1928* (London: Unwin Hyman, 1988).

—— *Blighty: British Society in the Era of the Great War* (London: Longman, 1996).

Dockrill, M. and J. D. Goold, *Peace without Promise: Britain and the Peace Conferences, 1919–23* (London: Batsford, 1981).

Douglas, R., 'The Background to the "Coupon" Election Agreements', *English Historical Review*, LXXXVI (1971), 318–36.

du Parcq, H., *Life of David Lloyd George*, 4 vols (London: Caxton, 1912–13).

Edwards, J. Hugh, *The Life of David Lloyd George*, 4 vols (London: Waverley Book Co., 1913).

Egerton, G. W., 'The Lloyd George *War Memoirs*: a Study in the Politics of Memory', *Journal of Modern History*, LX (1988), 55–94.

Fair, J., *British Inter-Party Conferences: a Study of the Procedure of Conciliation in British Politics, 1867–1921* (Oxford: OUP, 1980).

Fraser, D., *The Evolution of the British Welfare State* (London: Macmillan, 1973).

Freeden, M., *The New Liberalism* (Oxford: OUP, 1978).

French, D., *British Strategy and War Aims, 1914–16* (London: Allen & Unwin, 1986).

Gardiner, A. G., *Pillars of Society* (London: James Nisbet and Co., 1913).

Garside, W. R., *British Unemployment, 1919–39: a Study in Public Policy* (Cambridge: CUP, 1990).

George, W., *My Brother and I* (London: Eyre & Spottiswoode, 1958).

George, W. R. P., *The Making of Lloyd George* (London: Faber & Faber, 1976).

—— *Lloyd George: Backbencher* (Llandysul: Gomer Press, 1983).

Gilbert, B., *The Evolution of National Insurance in Great Britain* (London: Michael Joseph, 1966).

—— *David Lloyd George: the Architect of Change, 1863–1912* (London: Batsford, 1987).

—— 'David Lloyd George and the Great Marconi Scandal', *Historical Research*, LXII (1989), 295–317.

—— *David Lloyd George: Organizer of Victory, 1912–16* (London: Batsford, 1992).

Green, E., *The Crisis of Conservatism: the Politics, Economics and Ideology of the British Conservative Party* (London: Routledge, 1995).

Grieves, D., *The Politics of Manpower, 1914–18* (Manchester: Manchester University Press, 1988).

Grigg, J., *The Young Lloyd George* (London: Eyre Methuen, 1973)

—— *Lloyd George: the People's Champion, 1902–11* (London: Eyre Methuen, 1978).

—— *Lloyd George: from Peace to War, 1912–16* (London: Methuen, 1985).

Hart, M., 'The Decline of the Liberal Party in the Constituencies, 1914–31' (Oxford D.Phil., 1982).

Hazlehurst, C., *Politicians at War, July 1914 to May 1915: a Prelude to the Triumph of Lloyd George* (London: Cape, 1971).

Hazlehurst, C. and C. Woodland (eds.), *A Liberal Chronicle: Journals and Letters of J. A. Pease, 1st Lord Gainford, 1908–10* (London: Historians Press, 1994).

Jalland, P., *The Liberals and Ireland: the Ulster Question in British Politics to 1914* (Brighton: Harvester, 1980).

Jones, G. E., 'The Welsh Revolt Revisited: Merioneth and Montgomery in Default', *Welsh History Review*, XIV (1989), 417–37.

Jones, J. Graham, 'Alfred Thomas's National Institutions (Wales) Bills of 1891–2', *Welsh History Review*, XV (1990), 218–39.

Jones-Roberts, K. W., 'D. R. Daniel, 1859–1931', *Journal of the Merioneth History and Record Society*, V (1965), 58–77.

Kinnear, M., *The Fall of Lloyd George* (London: Macmillan, 1973).

Koss, S., 'Lloyd George and Nonconformity: the Last Rally', *English Historical Review*, LXXXIX (1974), 77–108.

Lentin, A., *Guilt at Versailles: Lloyd George and the Pre-History of Appeasement* (London: Methuen, 1985).

Liberal Land Committee, Rural Report, 1923–5, *The Land and the Nation* (London: Hodder & Stoughton, 1925).

Lloyd George, D., *Through Terror to Triumph* (London: Hodder & Stoughton, 1915).

—— *War Memoirs*, 2 vol. edn (London: Odhams, 1938).

—— *The Truth about the Peace Treaties*, 2 vols (London: Victor Gollancz, 1938).

Lloyd George, R., *Lloyd George* (London: Frederick Muller, 1960).

Loades, J., (ed.), *The Life and Times of David Lloyd George* (Bangor: Headstart History, 1991).

McEwen, J. M., 'The Struggle for Mastery in Britain: Lloyd George vs Asquith, December 1916', *Journal of British Studies*, XVIII (1978), 131–56.

—— 'Lloyd George's Liberal Supporters in December 1916: a Note', *Bulletin of the Institute of Historical Research*, LIII (1980), 265–72.

McKibbin, R., 'The Economic Policy of the Second Labour Government, 1929–31', *Past and Present*, LXVIII (1975), 95–123.

Matthews, K. G. P., 'Could Lloyd George have Done It?', *Oxford Economic Papers*, XLI (1989), 374–407.

Middleton, R., 'The Treasury and Public Investment: a Perspective on Inter-War Economic Management', *Public Administration*, LXI (1983), 351–70.

Morgan, K., 'Cardigan Politics: the Liberal Ascendancy, 1885–1923', *Ceredigion*, IV (1967), 311–46.

—— 'Wales and the Boer War – a Reply', *Welsh History Review*, IV (1969), 367–80.

—— 'Lloyd George and the Historians', *Transactions of the Honourable Society of Cymmrodorion* (1972), 65–85.

Morgan, K., *Lloyd George* (London: Weidenfeld & Nicolson, 1974).

—— *Consensus and Disunity: the Lloyd George Coalition Government, 1918–22* (Oxford: Clarendon, 1979).

—— *Rebirth of a Nation: Wales, 1880–1980* (Oxford: OUP, 1981).

—— 'Lloyd George and Germany', *Historical Journal*, XXXIX (1996), 755–66.

Morgan, K. (ed.), *Lloyd George: Family Letters, 1885–1936* (Cardiff and Oxford: University of Wales Press and OUP, 1973).

Morgan, K. and J., *Portrait of a Progressive: the Political Career of Christopher, Viscount Addison* (Oxford: Clarendon, 1980).

Murray, B., *The People's Budget, 1909/10: Lloyd George and Liberal Politics* (Oxford: OUP, 1980).

Nicolson, N. (ed.), *Harold Nicolson: Diaries and Letters*, 3 vols (London: Collins, 1966–8).

Owen, F., *Tempestuous Journey: Lloyd George, his Life and Times* (London: Hutchinson, 1954).

Packer, I., 'The Liberal Cave and the 1914 Budget', *English Historical Review*, CXI (1996), 620–35.

Pimlott, B. (ed.), *The Political Diary of Hugh Dalton, 1918–40, 1945–60* (London: Jonathan Cape, 1986).

Price, R. E., 'Lloyd George and Merioneth Politics 1885, 1886 – a Failure to Effect a Breakthrough', *Journal of Merioneth History and Record Society*, VIII (1975), 292–307.

Pugh, M., 'Asquith, Bonar Law and the First Coalition', *Historical Journal*, XVII (1974), 813–36.

—— *Lloyd George* (London: Longman, 1988).

Ramsden, J., *The Age of Balfour and Baldwin* (London: Longman, 1978).

Riddell, Ld, *An Intimate Diary of the Peace Conference and After, 1918–23* (London: Gollancz, 1933).

—— *More Pages From My Diary, 1908–14* (London: Country Life, 1934).

Roskill, S., *Hankey*, 3 vols (London: Collins, 1970–4).

Rowland, P., *Lloyd George* (London: Barrie & Jenkins, 1975).

Scally, R., *The Origins of the Lloyd George Coalition* (Princeton: Princeton University Press, 1975).

Searle, G., *Corruption in British Politics, 1895–1930* (Oxford: Clarendon, 1987).

—— *Country before Party: Coalition and the idea of 'National Government' in Modern Britain, 1885–1987* (London: Longman, 1995).

Sharp, A., *The Versailles Settlement: Peacemaking in Paris, 1919* (Basingstoke: Macmillan, 1991).

Skidelsky, R., *Politicians and the Slump* (London: Macmillan, 1967).

Smith, J., ' "Bluff, Bluster and Brinkmanship": Andrew Bonar Law and the Third Home Rule Bill', *Historical Journal*, XXXVI (1993), 161–78.

Spender, H., *The Prime Minister* (London: Hodder & Stoughton, 1920).

Spender, J. A. and C. Asquith, *Life of H. H. Asquith, Lord Oxford and Asquith*, 2 vols (London: Hutchinson, 1932).

Taylor, A. J. P. (ed.), *Lloyd George: Twelve Essays* (London: Hamish Hamilton, 1971).

—— *Lloyd George: a Diary by Frances Stevenson* (London: Hutchinson, 1971).

—— *My Darling Pussy: The Letters of Lloyd George and Frances Stevenson, 1913–41* (London: Weidenfeld & Nicolson, 1975).

Thorpe, A., 'The Industrial Meaning of "Gradualism": the Labour Party and Industry, 1918–31', *Journal of British Studies*, XXXV (1996), 84–113.

Turner, J., *British Politics and the Great War: Coalition and Conflict, 1915–18* (London and New Haven: Yale University Press, 1992).

Turner, J. (ed.), *Britain and the First World War* (London: Unwin Hyman, 1988).

Vincent, J., (ed.), *The Crawford Papers: the Journals of David Lindsay, 27th Earl of Crawford and 10th Earl of Balcarres, 1871–1940, during the years 1892 to 1940* (Manchester: Manchester University Press, 1984).

Williamson, P., *National Crisis and National Government: British Politics, the Economy and Empire, 1926–32* (Cambridge: CUP, 1992).

Wilson, J., *CB: A Life of Sir Henry Campbell-Bannerman* (London: Purnell Book Services, 1973).

Wilson, K. (ed.), *Decisions for War* (London: UCL Press, 1995).

Wilson, T., *The Downfall of the Liberal Party, 1914–35* (London: Fontana, 1968).

—— *The Myriad Faces of War* (Cambridge: Polity Press, 1988).

Wilson, T. (ed.), *The Political Diaries of C. P. Scott, 1911–28* (London: Collins, 1970).

Woodward, D. R., *Lloyd George and the Generals* (London: Associated University Press, 1983).

—— 'Did Lloyd George Starve the British Army of Men Prior to the German Offensive of March 1918 ?', *Historical Journal*, XXVII (1984), 241–52.

Wrigley, C., *Lloyd George* (Oxford: Blackwell, 1992).

Wrigley, C. (ed.), *A History of British Industrial Relations, 1914–39* (Brighton: Harvester, 1987).

INDEX